MW00584401

FINANCIAL STRATEGIES FOR PEOPLE OF ALL AGES
TO NAVIGATE THEIR GOLDEN YEARS WITH EASE

RETIRE
AND
REFIRE

ROBERT BARBERA

THE M
MENTORIS
PROJECT

Mentoris Project
745 South Sierra Madre Drive
San Marino, CA 91108

More information at www.mentorisproject.org

ISBN: 978-1-947431-49-2
Library of Congress Control Number: 2022940880

Publisher's Cataloging-in-Publication (Provided by Cassidy Cataloguing Services, Inc.)

Names: Barbera, Robert, 1932- author.
Title: Retire and refire : financial strategies for people of all ages to navigate their golden years with ease / Robert Barbera.
Description: San Marino, CA : The Mentoris Project, [2022]
Identifiers: ISBN: 9781947431492 (paperback) | 9798201227531 (ebook) | LCCN: 2022940880
Subjects: LCSH: Retirement income--Planning. | Retirees--Finance, Personal. | Finance, Personal. | Investments. | BISAC: BUSINESS & ECONOMICS / Personal Finance / Retirement Planning. | BUSINESS & ECONOMICS / Personal Finance / Investing. | BUSINESS & ECONOMICS / Personal Finance / Money Management.
Classification: LCC: HG179 .B37 2022 | DDC: 332.024014--dc23

CONTENTS

Introduction

This book was written to offer you some ideas of ways to improve your economic outlook in retirement. People in their thirties and forties are usually too busy earning a living and raising small children to think about their retirement, but that is a mistake. Meanwhile, people in their fifties, sixties, and seventies often think it's too late to do anything about their finances. That is also a mistake—a very costly one. This book was written to cover examples of each of these different age groups and show you how you can take action, no matter where you are in life, to improve your financial future.

Too often, we live in denial about what our retirement will look like. We don't want to think about it, or worse, we think we have no control over it, and so we don't take the time to evaluate it. Making an assessment of your financial situation can prevent unintended consequences and unpleasant shocks—and the earlier you do this, the better.

This is not meant to be a textbook, but rather an opportunity to see characters just like you, no matter what age you're starting at, learn to see their options and make more informed decisions regarding their retirement. This information is not intended to be a substitute for professional advice from experts. I'm not a lawyer or a financial advisor; I'm just someone who has thought a lot about how people can make the most of what they have, regardless of their stage of life. Do your own due diligence. Still, I hope you will find an enlightening perspective in this book.

Circumstances—our own, and those in the world around us—are

always changing. You have to commit to lifelong learning to keep up, and you have to be creative when thinking about solving the financial problems and setbacks you will inevitably face along the way. Knowledge is power, but so is common sense. Do the research. Use your own wisdom, accumulated during a lifetime of experience. Learn from others. And then it's up to you to make the best judgment for your own financial future.

I wish you a wonderful journey.

—Robert Barbera

Chapter One

ALL ABOARD

The Golden Years gleamed in the morning sunshine. St. Louis, Missouri, might be known as the "Gateway to the West," but for Joe and Betty Volpe, they hoped it would be the Gateway to Financial Freedom.

Joe and Betty were in their sixties and on the verge of retirement when they realized they didn't really have a plan for what that next step would look like. The riverboat *The Golden Years* promised a beautiful cruise down the Mississippi all the way to New Orleans, and while passengers enjoyed their days lounging on the river and exploring the towns and countryside along the way, they would also be learning about retirement options from a trio of financial wizards. This truly was to be the cruise of a lifetime—and one the couple hoped would set them up for a lifetime of financial security.

Betty could hardly contain her excitement as she and Joe crossed the gangplank.

"This is the best idea you've ever had," she told her husband.

"Not technically my idea," he answered. "You can thank Human Resources for the suggestion. When I started talking about retirement, they practically shoved the brochure into my hands."

"Well, I don't know how much we'll learn that we don't already know," Betty said, "but I do know how much fun we'll have in between the lectures. Did you see there's a spa on board?"

Joe grinned. "And a putting green. I can practice my game."

Betty gave his arm an affectionate squeeze. "You've only been retired a week and already you're in the swing of things." She glanced up and spotted a man waving from across the deck. "Look, there are Sam and Shirley! I'm so glad they decided to take the cruise, too. It'll be fun having someone to have dinner with."

"Don't forget, the point of this cruise is education. We're going to learn all we need to know about retirement."

"I'm already learning that retirement includes cruising, spas, and dinners I don't have to cook." Betty smiled up at her husband. "What more do I need to know?"

"There's so much we need to know," Shirley said, glancing at the day's program they'd been given on check-in. "We should have started thinking about retirement years ago."

"Shirley, relax." Her husband, Sam, waved one more time at Betty and Joe. Confident that they'd seen him, he turned to his wife. "That's why we're on this cruise—to learn what we need to do. There's still plenty of time."

"We're in our fifties, Sam."

"And we both love what we do. Neither one of us is ready to retire yet. We have time to make a plan and put it in place. Now come on, let's have some fun."

As they greeted their friends, Shirley noticed a woman working on her laptop in the business center. She nudged her husband. "Look, she's got to be ten years younger than us." Shirley sighed. "That's the right time to start thinking about retirement."

"We waited much too late to start thinking about retirement." Lamont sat on a chair across from his wife in the business center. "We should have started thinking about it in our thirties."

Gabriela finished her email and looked up at her husband. "We were too busy making stuff happen. I'm not convinced we should be here now."

"But we *are* here. So let's make the most of it, okay?"

Gabriela grinned. "Okay." She shut her laptop. "The business may crumble without me, but that is a small price to pay to get to be on a cruise with you."

Lamont smiled. "What about the chance to meet these financial gurus? I thought that was the draw."

"That's the bonus. Time with you is the draw." Gabriela slid her laptop into its case and together the couple headed out on deck. "Although I am looking forward to hearing the lectures."

She noticed an older woman leaning heavily on her cane, and came to her side.

"Oh, let me help you," Gabriela offered.

"Thank you," the woman replied. "I wanted to watch the shore as we got underway, but it was just a little too far from my chair to the handrail."

Gabriela took the woman's arm while Lamont gently guided her to the railing, where Betty and Joe were already standing with Sam and Shirley, looking out at the shore. They were just in time. The riverboat's engines kicked in and slowly, smoothly, the boat pulled away from the shore.

"Rose!"

They turned to see a gentleman in his early seventies heading toward them, a glass of iced tea in each hand. "There you are," he said. "I've been looking for you." He turned to Gabriela and Lamont. "Peter and Rose Yi. Nice to meet you."

He smiled at everyone and the four couples found themselves caught up in introductions. Betty's sharp eyes noticed that Rose was tiring.

"Why don't we all go into the salon?" Betty suggested. "We'll still get the spectacular views, but without the wind and engine noise."

Peter shot her a grateful look. The couples made their way inside and found some comfortable chairs.

Rose took a seat by the windows, facing forward. "Who would want to look back?" she laughed.

"We're certainly looking forward to this cruise," Shirley said. "There's so much we don't know about retirement."

The other couples nodded.

"It seems like so much advice is one-size-fits-all," Joe said. "I want to get to our one-on-one session."

"When do we meet the gurus?" Lamont asked.

Shirley pulled out her program and glanced at it. "In about two hours. In the auditorium. I guess they expect everyone to be there."

"We certainly will be," said Gabriela.

"Us as well," agreed Rose. "Although we may be late."

"Rose needs to rest up a bit," her husband explained. "It's been a tiring day."

"No worries," Lamont smiled. "We'll save you both a seat."

Suddenly, they were interrupted by the loudspeakers. They were being called to their check-in stations: It was time for the ship's muster drill.

"Do we have to?" asked Joe. "I was just getting comfortable."

"Sorry, sir," said a crewmember. "It's a mandatory safety drill. In case of emergency, we need to make sure everyone knows what to do to stay safe." He stood over them smiling but uncompromising. "If you would all go to your muster stations . . . ."

Everyone stood—Joe, a little reluctantly—and the group split up, with each couple going to the meeting area designated for their cabin. A different member of the crew led each safety orientation meeting, but the content was the same.

"Just as in a crowded theater," Captain Genevieve Olson explained to her group, "it's important to know where the exits are. Here, the exits happen to be lifeboats."

Shirley shuddered. "I don't even want to think about the boat going down, much less rehearse for it."

Sam shrugged. "I'd rather know how to survive it than pretend it could never happen."

His wife looked at him and smiled suddenly. "That's a metaphor for this whole trip, isn't it? Learning what we need to know in retirement so we don't go under?"

Sam grinned. "Could be, at that." He struggled to put on the Mae West life jacket a crewmember had handed out. "I just hope the clothing in our own golden years is a little more comfortable."

Meet Your Financial Gurus

After the safety drill, the couples went back to their cabins and rested a bit before gathering in the auditorium. As promised, Gabriela and Lamont had saved seats not just for Rose and Peter, but for the other couples as well. They gathered together and looked up expectantly at the stage. Three people, two men and a woman, came out of the wings to sit on three chairs in the middle of the stage, each person holding a microphone. They took a second to get settled as a stagehand set glasses of water on the low table between them. As the stagehand left, the blond man stood and moved to the center of the stage.

"Hello, everyone!" He grinned out at the packed auditorium. "Welcome to the Floating Financial Tour. We're going to be your guides and advisors as we navigate the waters of preparing for retirement—"

The woman interrupted him. "And you're going to hear a lot of bad nautical puns, especially from Gunnar. We can't stop him, but at least you've been warned."

Gunnar grinned. "This is Rachael, and part of her job is to keep you—and me—grounded in reality. There's a big difference between what you hope is true and what is really staring you in the face. Rachael has a gift when it comes to helping people see where they are and how to get to where they want to be."

Rachael gave a little wave to the audience.

"Rachael got her undergraduate degree at Emerson College and her MBA at The Wharton School," Gunnar continued. "She's been employed in several different companies in the financial world, beginning with a startup that helped people save more, and moving on to financial consulting, first for nonprofits and then ultimately for individuals. But her undergraduate degree is in psychology, not accounting. What really makes Rachael special is her ability to understand where people are coming from and why they make the decisions they do—which means she can help them make better decisions moving forward. Rachael?"

There was polite applause as she stood and took center stage. Gunnar sat back down and took a sip of water while Rachael addressed the crowd.

"One of the things I've learned," she said, "is that it can be a little uncomfortable to create an introduction for yourself. As you might have already guessed, we've decided to introduce each other instead. It's my pleasure to introduce you to the man who will be leading the educational portion of this cruise with daily lectures: William."

The dark-haired man waved. He wasn't as quick to smile as Gunnar had been, but he looked out over the crowd with kind eyes and a quiet manner.

"William got his undergraduate degree in economics at Yale and then got his master's at Harvard," Rachael continued. "He went on to work as a broker at major financial firms in New York. Now, that's a pretty good pedigree, but what really sets William apart is how passionate he is about helping people. Yes, he loves economics, and he is always learning, always trying to understand more and find better options to help people invest and save. But all of that comes from a place of genuinely wanting to help people live better, financially healthier lives. You will never meet anyone else as committed to helping you fulfill your financial dreams as William, and he's going to help you do it—even if it means making you take a hard look at some of the decisions you're currently making."

Someone in the audience spontaneously burst into applause and everyone else joined in. Even those who were a little concerned that they might have difficult decisions ahead felt that they were in safe hands.

William stood up as Rachael sat, and moved to the center of the stage.

"I hope very much that this trip will be the opportunity for you to learn a little about economics and a whole lot about yourself," he told them. "But first, let me have the pleasure of telling you a bit about my good friend, Gunnar. This is the last introduction before we get down to business, but definitely not the least. Gunnar is going to be leading the one-on-one sessions, which we call 'Reality Checks.' For some of you, they may be a bit of a jolt; for others, a pleasant surprise. But for everyone, there will need to be adjustments to make sure that not only you are financially ready for retirement, but mentally ready as well. First, let me tell you about Gunnar.

"Gunnar and I have been friends since the sixth grade. We grew up together just outside of Chicago, and he was always one of the smartest, nicest guys I knew. We took different paths when it came time for college. When you work with him, you'll realize Gunnar is a born teacher, and in fact he got his undergraduate degree at a small teaching college in Pennsylvania. He taught high school math for a few years, becoming somewhat obsessed with the question the kids kept asking: 'What will I ever use this for?'

"What Gunnar discovered was that no matter what he used as an example—engineering, computer science, sports—the one thing his kids were most interested in was, not surprisingly, money. But they also had the hardest time understanding some fundamental economic concepts. So Gunnar put his impressive brain to the task. He got a master's in education and eventually a PhD, doing his dissertation on strategies to help make money management more understandable to kids. Eventually, he turned to the even harder task of making it understandable to adults."

The crowd laughed.

"Round about that time," William continued, "my career was going well, I was a top producer, I had a corner office. But I found myself dissatisfied working for an investment bank. I wanted to focus on helping people understand the forces at work when it came to wealth building and management. I saw the work Gunnar was doing on the individual level and the idea for this company was born. We would offer cruises, guaranteeing us a captive audience, at least while we were on the water—"

"I don't know, William," Gunnar interrupted. "A few of them look like pretty strong swimmers." He winked at the audience and was rewarded with a laugh.

"We would offer cruises," William repeated firmly, "and I would teach the macroeconomics of wealth assessment while Gunnar would take on the microeconomics of people's individual situations with one-on-one Reality Checks. We were lucky enough to find Rachael, who would provide insight into why you make the decisions you do and how to make better ones. She also offers a woman's perspective. It's not that women and men innately make different money decisions, but it *is* true that they face different expectations and opportunities at home and in the workplace. The same life event—divorce being a prime example—can have the opposite impact on men that it does on women."

Gunnar and Rachael both stood at this and joined William at the front of the stage. He took a moment, surveying the crowd before speaking again.

"The fact that we are on this trip together is a dream come true for me," said William. "Here I am, able to work with my closest childhood friend and colleagues I respect, as we sail down this majestic river, the Mississippi. This journey is not unlike our own journey through life, and in particular our financial circumstances. There are constant changes in the river: Water levels rise and fall, there are bends in the river, corners you can't see around until you're past them, undercurrents you can't fathom, even times when it seems like you're doubling back and all forward momentum has been lost. It's all part of the journey."

He paused for a moment, letting his audience apply the metaphor to their own lives.

"I'm going to give you a look at the forces you can't control: national unemployment numbers, global war and peace, political decisions such as the Bretton Woods Agreement. Our own government departments, including the Federal Reserve, the Treasury, the Office of Management and Budget, the Internal Revenue Service, and the Department of Labor. Cycles of inflation, stagflation, recession, and depression. I want you to see the currents not because you can change them, but so you can learn to ride them.

"We're going to talk about the many strategies to consider in changing financial environments. We'll discuss the influence of economic theorists such as John Maynard Keynes and the need for a consistent analysis of the economy; Milton Friedman, on monetarist theory and individual responsibility; and Friedrich Hayek on how physical influences affect economic conditions. Rachael and Gunnar are going to help you see how these currents apply to you.

"I want you to see what forces are at play, but I also want you to be optimistic. It's important to note that we are on a ship that will bring us to our promised destination—in this case, the joy that is New Orleans. We hope our work with you sheds some light on how the country's finances influence us and how we can make our own decisions for a strong financial future. We can plan our navigation through changing conditions and we can start by doing our own Reality Check."

Reality Check: Oliver and Priyanka

Gunnar signaled to the projectionist and the lights dimmed. On a screen behind him, there appeared a photo of a happy couple in their forties.

"Meet Oliver and Priyanka," Gunnar began. "They are good friends of mine who agreed to be our experimental subjects when William and I began developing our Reality Check. They filled out the same form that each of you will find in your cabins tonight. Here are some of the questions we asked."

He clicked a remote and the next slide appeared behind him.

"What are your assets? Of course there's the balance in your bank accounts, but beyond that. Do you own your car or are you still paying it off? How much equity do you have in your home? What about your furniture? Collections? Clothing? Do you have a stock portfolio? Pensions? IRA accounts? Any rental properties? How about your debts: mortgages, credit cards, car payments, notes and guarantees? What are your sources of income?

"Don't panic—you don't need to answer these right this minute. We're going to provide you with the full list of questions. We want you to be exhaustive. Get as complete a picture as possible of where you stand financially at this moment. Most of you, maybe all of you, will end up being surprised—but I'm afraid only a few will find it a pleasant surprise.

"Perhaps the most important question you can ask yourself is: What do you actually want your retirement to look like? What are your expectations? Do you have any goals you want to reach? Any bucket-list items you want to do? If you're part of a couple, you need to have a serious conversation about what each of you wants. Don't assume that just because you want to travel the world, your partner will as well."

He clicked the remote again and began to take the audience through Oliver and Priyanka's Reality Check.

> Oliver is forty-six. He works at an auto dealership Monday through Friday as the manager of their service department. He's off on Saturdays, but he came up the ranks as a mechanic and he really loves cars. On Saturdays, he works for a local company that leases cars, maintaining their engines. His annual take-home pay is $65,000 from his primary job and another $10,000 from his Saturday work.

> Priyanka is forty-five and is an administrative assistant at a large manufacturing company. Her net income is $40,000 a year. Both have pension plans provided by their employers. Their two sons are in college and carrying moderate student loans. They're a sandwich-generation family, helping out both sets of parents physically and financially, as well as their sons. Like most Americans, they have very little in savings. A study published in 2020 found that one-third of Americans have $1,000 or less in savings, and Oliver and Priyanka are no exception.

"When they filled out our questionnaire, they realized that by the time Oliver is fifty-five, they will have paid off the debt on their house. If they also start saving aggressively, including the income from Oliver's second job and any additional bonuses and raises, they can expect to have the following to retire."

Gunnar brought up the final series of slides.

SAVINGS ACCUMULATED OVER 9 YEARS

Saturday earnings ($10,000/year)	$90,000
10% of family budget from annual combined salaries	$94,500
TOTAL SAVINGS	**$184,500**

(Note that this does not include what they could be earning by investing their savings.)

"We're assuming a thirty-year retirement window. Were they, at retirement, to invest this money in a diverse portfolio, they could expect to draw an annual income from it each year over those thirty years. The amount they can withdraw and still have the money last thirty years will depend on their rate of return. For instance:"

INTEREST RATE ON $184,500 SAVINGS ACCUMULATED FROM AGES 30–85	POTENTIAL ANNUAL WITHDRAWAL
6%	$13,400
8%	$16,389
10%	$19,572

"Obviously, even without a mortgage, they wouldn't be able to manage on their savings alone. Luckily, both have employer-sponsored pensions. Oliver has worked for the auto dealership most of his adult life, and while Priyanka has changed employers several times, she has been able to roll over her pension."

Oliver's projected annual pension income at age 55: $45,000	
Priyanka's projected annual pension income at age 55: $20,000	
Total projected annual pension earnings	$65,000
Income from savings (using the 8% figure above)	$16,389
TOTAL RETIREMENT INCOME (BEFORE TAXES)	**$81,389**

Gunnar signaled for the lights to come back up and turned to his audience.

"While $80,000-plus a year looks like a healthy figure," he said, "remember that Oliver and Priyanka are currently struggling to save money on a combined income of $115,000 a year. Their projected retirement income is significantly less, and if they give into the temptation to take more out of their savings—for a vacation, say, or to help with a son's wedding—they will have to live on even less as they get older.

"And as I mentioned earlier, Oliver and Priyanka are a sandwich generation. They are going to want to help their sons get started in life, and just about the time they plan to retire, their boys may be starting families of their own, perhaps looking to buy their first house. Meanwhile both Oliver and Priyanka's parents already have some health and mobility issues and are needing more time and attention, a burden that primarily falls on Priyanka as Oliver works at least part of every weekend.

"On one hand, Oliver and Priyanka were relieved to see that they wouldn't be destitute. With their mortgage paid off, that would be one financial burden they wouldn't be carrying into retirement, and if they had to downsize, the money from the sale of their house would significantly bolster their savings. On the other hand, the reality that they would be living on only three-quarters of the income they currently enjoy brought them up short."

There was some uncomfortable movement in the audience as many people realized they would be in a similar situation themselves.

Gunnar smiled. "Don't despair. There are options. First, they don't have to retire at fifty-five. Right? It could be that simple. To keep working even an extra couple of years would increase their savings. As I mentioned earlier, they could intentionally downsize their life. They don't necessarily have to sell their house; they could rent it out. This is a particularly attractive option if their own parents need so much help that they have to move in with them for a year or two. This isn't an option for everyone, but both Oliver and Priyanka have very close relationships with their parents and in-laws, and it's a solution that could benefit everyone.

"Part-time work is another option. Even if Oliver were to only continue his Saturday side job, that's an extra $10,000 a year they could count on. And Priyanka has been invaluable to her employer, particularly at tax time when she has taken on a lot of the financial prep work that no one else wanted to do. It's quite possible her employer would be delighted to pay her to come in one day a week or even to work full-time for six weeks in March and April, just to take care of their books.

"The reality is that each of these strategies would help, and all of them together would give my friends a lot more flexibility in retirement.

"One thing we haven't mentioned—and which ultimately helped Oliver and Priyanka decide to delay retirement until they reached their sixties—is health insurance. They both have good medical insurance on their employers' plans, and with the emotional demands of their families, the last thing they needed was the pressure of paying for health insurance in those years between retirement and being eligible for Medicare.

"This may sound like they were pressured into staying in the workforce, but actually, that decision—which made sound financial sense to them—also gave them enormous relief. It felt like an overwhelming sprint to save enough over the next nine years and to face the massive change of retirement right at a time when they knew both their parents and their children would be needing even more from them emotionally and possibly financially. Oliver and Priyanka both enjoy their jobs, and as we'll learn later on the cruise, staying active and engaged is incredibly important, not just to your quality of life, but also to your actual life expectancy.

"But the single most important change they made after our Reality Check was to start saving aggressively. You need to change your mindset: You are not working for a paycheck, and you're definitely not working just to pay your bills.

"You are working for capital.

"That shift in mindset changes everything. When you're working for capital, you are committed to taking that capital and investing it so your money starts working for you. It's the difference between stuffing money under the mattress and slowly accumulating and dispersing it versus building something with it that will continue to generate funds long after you've retired. There are many different ways to invest and we will go over many of them in the coming days.

"In the meantime, start shifting your own mindset. And while you're at it, enjoy yourselves. We mean that. This is your life we're talking about; the journey needs to be as fulfilling and joyful as possible."

"I want to second that." William joined Gunnar and looked out at the audience. "Too often, we think of saving for retirement as a chore, as something difficult and unpleasant. And yes, sometimes deferring a new car or a vacation while you get your safety net in place can be disheartening. But the answer isn't to be miserable now so that you can be secure later."

Rachael jumped in. "The answer is not to blow it all now, either." She smiled. "Not being secure later also leads to a lot of misery."

"Right." William took a minute to really look at everyone in the audience.

Shirley, from her seat next to Sam, got chills; she felt William was looking straight into her heart when he spoke.

"What we want you to do is be creative about how you build your future," William continued. "We want you to see the possibilities so you can live a happy, fulfilling life now AND have guardrails in place to keep you on track to an equally happy and fulfilling retirement. The journey is the destination. Have a great trip!"

William smiled as Gunnar gave a mock bow to the crowd and Rachael waved as the crowd applauded. The lights came up and the audience began to disperse. Everyone had a feeling of possibility and excitement as they headed for the decks.

They were on their way.

Dinner: All You Can Eat

Dinner that night was traditional American fare, buffet style. Peter and Rose had arranged to meet up with Gabriela and Lamont; they sat at a table overlooking the water.

16

"Is everything on this trip meant to be a metaphor?" Lamont asked.

"What do you mean?" asked Peter.

"Look at us." He gestured to each of their plates. "We've all taken a little something different from the buffet—salads, steaks, potatoes, soups, veggie burgers, fruit. Doesn't it seem like, with all the information we're going to get on this trip, we'll each be choosing what works best for us?"

Rose smiled. "That makes it sound much more delightful than scrimping and saving every penny."

"They did say we were supposed to enjoy the journey," Gabriela agreed. "Speaking of which, that dessert tray is calling my name!"

Reality Check

Your Financial Questionnaire

Start with your assets:

- How much money is in your checking account? Your savings account?
- How much can you expect in Social Security? The website ssa.gov has tools to help you estimate how much you can expect monthly.
- Do you have a pension plan through your employer? (Note: If you do, and you have not yet taken advantage of it, do so right now—especially if your employer will match your contribution.) How much can you expect annually from your pension?
- What about retirement savings? How much is in your IRA (Traditional and/or Roth) or your 401(k) or 403(b)?
- How much is in your stock portfolio? Other investment accounts? Annuities?
- What's your current equity in your home?
- Are there any life insurance policies that list you as the beneficiary?
- Do you own any rental properties?
- Are any royalties coming in from books or other projects?
- Do you have any trust income?
- What about other assets: your car, furniture/furnishings, clothing, collections? What are they worth?
- If you own your own business or practice, what is it worth?
- What are your current income sources? List everything, including side hustles.
- Is there anything else you can think of that is an asset?

Now for your debts:

- Mortgage
- Student loans
- Credit cards
- Medical debt
- Notes
- Guarantees
- Do you owe money anywhere else?

It's also a good idea to take a look at your monthly expenses. How much are you spending every month?

- Groceries
- Medicines/medical bills
- Clothing
- Education (for yourself or a dependent)
- Entertainment
- Utilities
- Property taxes (How much do you need to set aside monthly to make your annual payment?)
- Self-employment taxes
- Is there anything else you spend money on every month? How much?

Chapter Two

THE RIGHT QUESTIONS

The Morning Ritual

The morning dawned cool and clear. Before embarking, Joe and Sam had made a pact to walk eight laps of the third deck every morning, just to make sure they were up and enjoying every minute of the trip—and maybe to walk off a little of the excellent food they were being served. They had invited Lamont and Peter to join them, and the four men set out at a brisk pace. They were soon lapped by Gabriela, who was jogging the same track. She gave them a cheery wave and went on, enjoying the music playing in her ear buds.

Meanwhile, the other three women had decided to check out the Tai Chi class in the glassed-in spa area. The views were spectacular, and the graceful movements of the Tai Chi almost made them feel like they were gliding through life. The instructor helped Rose modify the workout so that she was able to do the stretches from a chair. There was a contentment in the air, and at the same time, a definite energy: Everyone was looking forward to what the day would bring.

The couples met back up after their morning exercise for breakfast.

"So what did you boys talk about?" Betty asked.

"Mostly how glad we were to be on vacation," Joe replied. "What about you all?"

"The same," Shirley replied. "It's funny—I would never have said I was in a rut at home, but even being away for just a day, I'm starting to see how locked into my routine I am."

"What is it you do, Shirley?" asked Peter.

"I manage a stationery store and gift shop," she answered. "In fact, that's how Sam and I met. The store had belonged to my parents. I was working there over the summer after college and Sam showed up one day as the new sales rep for a novelty company we often stocked gifts from."

"Love at first sight," Sam said proudly.

"When my folks retired, I took over the family store, but Sam liked being a sales rep."

"I don't love the traveling," Sam clarified.

"No, but you like the people," his wife replied. "Sales is all about relationships and that's why you're so good at it. You take the time to get to know people, you know the kinds of things each store manager likes to stock, and you don't spam them with items just because you make a commission."

"I do like talking to people," Sam admitted. "I feel lucky that I've been able to build a career doing something I really enjoy."

"What about you, Shirley?" Rose asked gently. "Do you enjoy running the gift shop?"

Shirley hesitated. "I don't dislike it. When our kids were little, being my own boss gave me a lot of flexibility. We have a great staff, and over the years the shop has really become a reflection of my personality. I like it a great deal more than if I were only a hired hand!"

"There's nothing like running your own business," Peter agreed. "Even when you have to make hard decisions, at least you understand the whole picture. You're actively making choices, not having things happen to you by the Powers That Be and struggling to understand them."

"Tell me about it!" Betty laughed. "I've been a schoolteacher my entire career. I can run my classroom as I see fit—most of the time, anyway! But communication between my school's administration and the teachers isn't always clear. Which is very frustrating because I'm an English teacher! Clear communication is what I teach every day!"

"There's good and bad on both sides," Lamont said. "I'm a graphic designer. I'm employed part-time by a small, local advertising agency, and I like the stability of the work. And they withhold money for my taxes and pay into Social Security, which is great. But I also run my own freelance business on the side, doing graphic design for a variety of clients, and that has a plus side, too. I can do the work on my own time, I can turn down work from clients who end up being impossible to please, and I also like the fact that every project is a new challenge. But as a freelancer, tax time is a hassle!"

"Hey," Joe said, finishing his coffee, "we'd better get cracking. William's lecture is about to start."

LECTURE 1: THE RIGHT QUESTIONS

They reached their seats just in time. William was already onstage, a glass of water on a small table by his side.

"Welcome back, everyone," he began. "Today, we're going to talk about the first step toward having not just a secure retirement, but also one that's filled with wealth, both in monetary terms and in quality of life. And no, it's not going to be the stock market or cryptocurrency or any of the other flashy wealth-building options that make for great headlines or clickbait. No, the first step isn't glamorous, but it is critical.

"You have to ask yourself the right questions."

He paused for a second to let everyone take that in. Betty had her laptop open; she was typing even as she listened intently. Gabriela and Sam were both taking notes on legal notepads the ship had provided.

William took a sip of water and continued. "You have to be willing to look at where you are. I mean, that should be obvious. You have to sit with the numbers: How much in savings? How much in pensions and IRA portfolios? How much in stocks, which can grow faster but are also more volatile, and how much in slower-growing assets that you can tap into when the market is down and it's not smart to sell? How much value is in your house? What about other assets? You need to take full, clear-eyed stock of your financial situation. This is something our Reality Check hopes to help you with. You received the full questionnaire yesterday.

"But you also need to ask questions about the future. Where do you want to live in retirement? Are you planning to move to a different community? Do you want to keep living in your house or do you want to downsize? What about travel? People think, oh, when I'm not working, I won't need to commute, I won't need business clothes, so I won't need as much money. That, by and large, is not true. Sure, you won't be spending money on the same things you were spending on during your working years, but you'll hopefully be doing other things, like traveling to see the world or visiting family or taking the grandkids on vacation. Exploring new hobbies or long-delayed dreams. And inflation is always looming—things will always cost more over time. You don't want to just exist for the next thirty years; you want to enjoy your time and really live.

"For that, you need to ask yourself—and your partner, if you're a couple—some pretty foundational questions.

"First, what are some things you want to do in retirement? Do you have a goal? Probably you do. We human beings are hardwired for goals. Even if you think all you want to do is hang out a 'Gone Fishing' sign every day, that's a goal. It takes a level of financial security to make that happen.

"And you probably have other goals," William added. "Traveling is a common one, but so is writing your memoirs, learning to paint watercolors, or pursuing any hobby or lifelong passion. The thing is, you probably haven't decided—intentionally—how you're going to incorporate that into your retirement. And that is a big mistake.

"First, of course, is the problem of communication. If you're part of a couple, you may not realize that you both have different visions for the last third of your life. I hope all of you have at least thirty years in retirement, or roughly as long a life out of the workforce as you had in it. Some couples simply assume they each know what the other wants to do and are surprised to learn they have entirely different ideas: One wants to travel, the other one wants to build a dream home or move to be near grandchildren or go back to school. There is nothing wrong with any of these dreams. One is not morally better than another. You just don't want to discover them after your retirement party is over.

"The second problem is that, if you haven't deliberately thought about your retirement, you might slide into simply doing nothing. Oh, you may get dressed in the morning, but that's about it. As you're flailing around, trying to fill your days, you may also become depressed. Those long-cherished dreams that are in the back of your mind have no chance to come to fruition if you won't even acknowledge them. This lack of planning can be fatal—and I don't mean that metaphorically.

"As human beings, we need a sense of purpose. Men who have their whole identity wrapped up in their career—where they may have come to rely on the respect they get from others and the ego boost of a job well done—may suddenly be plagued by feelings of incompetence once they no longer have that environment where they can shine. They may start feeling old and useless, and the body doesn't respond well to this. A lot of men develop health problems within a couple of years of retiring, and too many don't live very long into what should be their golden years.

"Obviously, many of those studies were done on men during a time when, culturally, men were the primary breadwinners, but the same is true for women. Whether it's that your children are now grown and living their own lives, so your identity as a mother feels threatened, or the advertising agency you helped establish sends you into retirement with a big going-away party and suddenly you have no new accounts to wow with your creativity, any change in life that disrupts your sense of identity can lead to real, and sometimes dire, health issues. We think we just want to take it easy and sleep in. Really, no matter where we are in our lives, we want to feel connected and valuable.

"Acknowledging this and putting a plan in place before your identity shifts in retirement and your world is turned upside down—that's as important as planning for your financial well-being. Having the money in place to live well for the next thirty years only matters if you're going to be around to enjoy it."

THE VALUE OF PLANNING

After William's lecture, the men went to grab some lunch and explore the ship. Joe and Peter decided to golf, while Lamont went skeet shooting and Sam read the newspaper on deck. The women, however, had more learning to do: Rachael was hosting a British high tea in the lounge. Most of the women on board decided to go there instead of helping themselves at the buffet lunch.

"The tea is a lure!" Rachael laughed as the women took their seats. "I've discovered that finger sandwiches and scones with clotted cream make even the driest lecture more fun. And that's our theme, right? Enjoy the journey."

"If all journeys included tea," Gabriela said, "I would be much more likely to leave home." She sat with Betty, Shirley, and Rose at one of the café tables that had been set up for the event. Pots of tea were placed at every table while waiters with rolling carts offered the women tiny sandwiches, scones, jams, and desserts.

"Do you not like to travel?" Betty asked, trying some clotted cream on her scone.

"I do," Gabriela replied. "But I run my own business and there are always fires to put out. I feel guilty spending time away from the office."

"I had to schedule both of my assistant managers to cover me this week," Shirley laughed. "I had no idea how much work I gave myself to do until I realized I couldn't possibly have just one person try to do it all while I'm gone."

Rachael had stopped by their table and overheard Shirley. "That is the perfect segue for my lecture," she said. "Hold that thought while I get started."

Rachael went to the front of the room. "While you are all enjoying your tea," she said, "I want to talk to you about the single most important concept in having a successful retirement. And happily, it's something you're all already expert in."

"I bet it's multitasking," whispered Betty to her friends.

"You know the old saying," replied Rose. "If you want something done, ask a busy woman."

Rachael looked over at them and winked. "It's preparation," she said. "Planning ahead. Thinking about what could go wrong, and what you'll do to prevent or at least mitigate potential problems.

"How do I know you're all expert at this?" she continued. "Because you're all here. Look what you had to do to get here.

"First, you had to find this cruise. We don't have flashy TV ads; almost everyone who comes here was referred to us by a friend or by their Human Resources department. Which means you are someone with a strong network and/or someone who utilizes the resources available to them, like H.R. And you're not too proud to take good advice when it's offered. That's a tremendously undervalued skill, but one that can change your life.

"Many of you had to organize your work to be able to take time off. You had to delegate, provide coverage, maybe finish some projects ahead of schedule. If you didn't have a team in place, people you trust, you would never have been able to be here today. The same is true if you're someone who has to micromanage every detail. But you do have a competent, trustworthy team and you were able to let go and let others step up to the plate, so here you are.

"Whether or not you had to organize your work to survive without you for a couple of weeks, you definitely had to organize your personal life to keep going. Some of you needed to find childcare, maybe even organizing a wonderful trip for your kids to visit their grandparents or a favorite aunt and uncle while you're gone—a trip you won't even be taking with them. If you don't have kids or they're older and have already flown the nest, you still had to take care of a hundred mundane details that would have caused problems if they weren't addressed. For instance, you may have had to prepay bills, stop the mail, get a cat sitter, buy luggage, and let your friends or family or the places you volunteer know that they won't be seeing you for a little while. You may have imagined what it might be like on a cruise and packed or even purchased appropriate clothes. Maybe you even did some research, looking up the typical weather on the Mississippi this time of year or reading cruise reviews online, maybe checking out some fun things to do in our ports of call. You all put your intelligence to work, coupled with time and effort, to make this trip enjoyable and smooth.

"So here's my question to you: Why would you expect to launch into what will hopefully be a multidecade phase of your life—your retirement, your golden years—without putting at least as much effort into it as you would going on a two-week vacation?"

Rachael paused a moment to let everyone take that in. Shirley raised her hand.

"If I thought of it that way, of course I wouldn't," Shirley answered. "The problem is, I don't really think about it at all. I'm too busy dealing with the day-to-day—all of those things you mentioned. I have to make sure that and more is taken care of on a daily basis."

Rachael smiled. "Of course you do. That's really my point. You are capable of taking care of everything once you turn your attention to it. And now, you are turning your attention to preparing for your retirement. You have already taken the hardest step.

"Everything we do with you this week is meant to show you the need for planning and to give you many different ways to think about your future. I want you to know you are already good at this. No matter where you are in life, there are steps you can take to make your retirement situation stronger and the transition smoother. Putting your creativity to the task will help you brainstorm solutions, and your already well-honed ability to get things done means that you will be able to implement those solutions.

"Here's the last thing I want to say, and then I'll let you get back to this lovely tea: Things may still go wrong." She paused, looking out over the room with a gentle smile. "Not what you expected me to say, was it?" Rachael gave a little shrug. "It doesn't serve us to pretend that bad things don't happen. Markets crash, fires rage, and we can't always count on our plans coming to fruition. So why make a plan at all? Because if we don't, we are all but guaranteed to find ourselves floundering in the future, desperately trying to cobble together the life we want—without really having thought about what that might look like.

"When we do plan, even if the plan goes wrong, we have spent time thinking about what we want and why we want it. Even when the "how we get there" gets thrown out the window, we can regroup so much more quickly when we have a goal in mind. Life doesn't just happen to us; we take charge of our future. And even when things go awry, we can sleep better knowing that we did what we could to put ourselves on the path to success."

As the women finished their tea, Gabriela looked thoughtful. "I am spending all my energy working to grow my business now," she told her new friends. "I guess I just thought as long as my business is thriving, I don't really have to worry about retirement. It'll just take care of itself."

Betty shook her head. "I thought the same thing because I have a pension. But let me tell you, retirement time is coming up fast and I have never felt so unprepared."

"Peter and I did a good job of planning financially," Rose told them. "We had both started setting money aside in our individual IRA accounts many years ago, before we'd even met. But we never sat down and talked about our retirement in terms of what we wanted our life to look like, the kinds of things we wanted to do. How to make our lives bigger, rather than smaller, after we retired—that would have been a good conversation to have," she added.

Shirley nodded. "Sam and I need to have that conversation as well. I've always wanted to travel, but he's on the road for work so much that he'd rather stay close to home when we do get time off. This trip was a real rarity for us. I have to say," she added with a smile, "I am relieved that any plan is better than no plan. I may not be able to make the perfect plan, but I can for sure put something in place."

"We can all do that much," Gabriela agreed as they finished up their tea. "And you're right, it feels so much better to do a little planning now rather than stressing over being perfect—or worse, regretting not having done anything ten or twenty years from now."

Spin the Wheel

Later that afternoon, *The Golden Years* docked at its first port of call, the highlight of which was a local riverboat casino. The casino was alive with bells and whistles; bright lights flashed in a variety of colors.

Peter and Rose were dressed to the nines. "We're taking advantage of every chance we can get to be fancy," Rose announced to Gabriela and Lamont, who had also dressed up for the occasion. She had a cane with her, and even that had been bedazzled with rhinestones. "No tiara," she lamented, "but at least my cane sparkles." She and Peter toured the card tables until Rose tired; after that, they sat at the bar and watched the crowds of people play.

Betty and Joe took a quick tour as well, but soon settled in at the slot machines. Betty was happy to keep playing them, but Joe quickly got bored and moved over to the Texas Hold'em poker tables.

Lamont and Gabriela spent some time in the bar enjoying cocktails and live music coming from a tiny stage. When the band took a break, the couple tried their hand at the roulette wheel and the blackjack table. Peter joined Lamont at Texas Hold'em while Gabriela joined Rose at a table by the stage as the band started their next set.

Shirley and Sam helped themselves to the all-you-can-eat buffet before starting in at the video poker machines. They moved on to the actual poker tables, splitting up to play blackjack and Mississippi Stud.

All the couples lost track of time as they won and lost and won and lost some more. It wasn't until crewmembers from *The Golden Years* reminded them that the ship would be leaving shortly, with or without them, that everyone was able to pry themselves away from the delights the casino had to offer.

Music of the Night

Back aboard their own ship, Peter and Rose went straight to bed, but the other three couples felt too restless to go back to their cabins. Instead, they discovered that the piano bar had a trio of singers doing a set of Broadway tunes. Happily, they settled in to listen.

When the soprano belted out "I Cain't Say No" from *Oklahoma!*, Shirley smiled ruefully. She couldn't help but think of their time in the casino. She and Sam had been up eighty dollars at one point, but then ended up losing just over two hundred dollars that night, largely because they couldn't say no to just one more hand. When the tenor followed up with "Ya Got Trouble" from *The Music Man*, Shirley almost laughed out loud.

When the singers began the eponymous duet from *Sunday in the Park with George*, it was Lamont's turn to be thoughtful. The musical is about creating art, as well as balancing that art with the rest of your life—something he had been struggling with. Retirement seemed very far away, but he realized he didn't want to spend the years between now and then only working as a graphic artist for other people's projects. "Enjoy the journey," he reminded himself.

The show ended with all of the performers singing "Tomorrow" from *Annie*.

"This must be the most optimistic song ever to grace a Broadway stage," whispered Betty to Joe.

He grinned. "Everything here really is designed to make us think about the future," Joe whispered back. "At least this song is hopeful about it!"

Chapter Three

DON'T GAMBLE ON YOUR FUTURE

The Morning Ritual

The men met for another tour of the ship's track early in the morning. The cool breeze was refreshing and there was an air of excitement, especially because the first couple among the group was going to get to sit down with Gunnar today for their Reality Check.

"I have to admit, I'm a little nervous," said Sam. "I'm sure there are a thousand things we've never even thought about."

"It's good that they're thorough," Peter told him. "You may not even know what questions to ask going in, but you're going to walk out with marching orders."

In the spa area, Gabriela joined the other women for their Tai Chi class. "Usually, I don't feel like I'm exercising unless I'm running," she told them afterward, "but this was fun."

Rose laughed. "Don't kid yourself," she said to Gabriela. "The movements may have been small and controlled, but you used muscles you may not even know you have."

"I'll bet I did!" Gabriela laughed as the women went for coffee in the lounge. "I'm sure I'll feel it tomorrow."

"There's another metaphor for us," Betty pointed out. "Just like in Tai Chi, small, controlled movements add up over time to create big results."

"Can I borrow that idea?"

The women looked up to see Rachael by the coffee station.

"I'm always looking for new ways to explain what we're trying to do here," she added, "and that one is a doozy!"

"Won't you join us?" invited Shirley.

"Thanks, I'd love to." Rachael brought her mug over and pulled up a chair. "How are you enjoying the cruise so far?"

"It's the trip of a lifetime," Shirley assured her.

Rachael looked pleased. "Let me know if you have any questions. One of my jobs is to wander about, making myself available for informal questions. So please, feel free."

"Is your job on the team particularly to talk to women?" Gabriela asked.

Rachael nodded. "Partly," she answered. "William is really a sweetie, but he can seem a bit intimidating. Men generally go to Gunnar with questions, and nearly everyone gets a chance to talk to him one-on-one, but his focus is on specific action plans to get people from where they are to where they need to be. Everyone needs someone they feel comfortable talking to, and for some women, it's easier to have this kind of conversation with another woman."

"You are very easy to talk to," Betty said.

Rachael smiled. "Thank you. So are you. I love this part of my job. Do any of you have any questions for me? Shirley? You're looking thoughtful."

"Well . . . ." Shirley was quiet for a moment before continuing. "I'm a little embarrassed to say, but I hate thinking about bad things happening in the future. It makes me upset to think about things like 'What if my gift shop goes under?' or 'What if Sam has a heart attack?' But it seems to me like planning for our retirement is going to involve a lot of me thinking about worst-case scenarios."

"I don't think that's anything to be embarrassed about," Betty put in. "No one likes to think about terrible 'what-ifs.' I know I don't!"

"And you're not wrong," Rachael told Shirley. "We are going to make you look at some future scenarios that we all hope won't happen.

But the truth is, you're going to think about those things anyway—usually late at night, when you should be getting some rest."

Shirley laughed. "It's like you've known me for years!"

"Surprise! You're human." Rachael smiled. "It's just as Betty said. No one likes to think of those things. But we're going to ask you to think about them now and then put a plan in place that will, if not prevent them, at least mitigate the damage to your life. Once that plan is in place, a lot less of your mental energy needs to go toward worrying about the future. You can tell yourself, 'Hey, it's okay, I have a plan.' And sometimes, when something new happens, good or bad—an opportunity or a windfall or a setback—you can revisit your plan and adjust it as needed. But that's a far cry from having no plan at all. You don't need to feel tossed about by the winds of chance; you have some safeguards in place to anchor you no matter what else is going on."

"It's just like the safety drill we did on the first day, isn't it?" Shirley asked. "I told Sam then that it was a metaphor for this trip—learning what could go wrong, not to scare us, but so we have a plan in place for what to do if disaster did strike. We wouldn't be caught off guard and left to founder. Of course, I was half joking at the time," she added.

"But that's it exactly!" answered Rachael. "You were right on, Shirley. Just as it's important to have a safety drill—Where's the best exit? Where's a backup exit? How do you put on your life vest properly? Where are those darn lifeboats?—it's important to have something like that for your life. Do you have savings you can tap into easily and without penalty to keep you going for six months if something happens and you have to put your financial life back together? Most Americans don't have enough in savings to cover an unexpected $1,000 financial emergency. Many car repairs can cost nearly that much, and a lot of us are dependent on our cars to get to work, so it can become a vicious cycle very quickly. Having even a small emergency savings as a cushion can keep an inconvenience from becoming a disaster.

"The same is true in your retirement. Knowing how much is available to you every month and from where allows you to plan and budget. Having some money set aside that you can tap into without penalty—that's your first lifeboat. Maybe having a Plan B in place for a real emergency. Can you rent out your house and live with your kids for a year?

Can you downsize by selling your house and moving to someplace smaller, maybe rented, maybe to an area with a lower cost of living? How might you be able to right the ship? Having a backup plan allows you the physical and mental space to regroup and is far less stressful than trying to find creative solutions while you're living through a crisis."

At that moment, the men entered the lounge. Rachael excused herself and went to sit with another group, leaving all of the women with much to think about and discuss with their partners. But there was no time to do either right now. William's next lecture was about to start.

LECTURE 2: DON'T GAMBLE ON YOUR FUTURE

As everyone settled into their seats, William watched them from his vantage point onstage. He looked more serious than he had the day before, and Joe found himself a little uncomfortable as William's gaze fell on their group.

"So how was the riverboat casino last night?" William asked.

Most of the crowd applauded; some of the younger men whooped in appreciation, while a few other people shook their heads in regret. William waited for the noise to subside.

"I heard some of you had a hard time leaving," he said finally. "In fact, I heard that some of you had to be warned that the ship would leave without you before you could be pried away from the tables and machines. Luckily, you all made it back in time. No harm done, right?" He paused for a moment. No one answered. "Right. No long-term harm done because we created some guardrails for you. We had shuttles to bring you back to the ship, text reminders to warn you when to start heading back, and crewmembers whose job was to make sure you didn't, quite literally, miss the boat.

"Without those guardrails that we set in place, some of you might have reached the dock only to find this ship had sailed. It would have cost you time, money, and a great deal of inconvenience to get yourselves to our next port of call in time to reboard. Some of you may have stayed or even gone back to continue gambling, and inevitably a few would have lost more than they could afford."

Some members of the audience began to squirm.

"Let me be clear," William continued. "I have nothing against responsible gambling. On the contrary, I find nothing immoral about going to a riverboat casino. The live shows can be great fun, the food is often justifiably renowned, and people have been playing games of chance for money for thousands of years. Who am I to object?

"But it's an event that can cause one to lose control, and that is always something to be wary of. Remember that everything about a casino, from the bright lights and the sounds of jackpots to the lack of clocks so you can't easily keep track of time—everything in a casino has been designed to keep you there. So if you're going to go, you need to have an exit strategy in place.

"Decide ahead of time how much you're willing to lose. Bring only that much in cash. Don't bring your credit card, or if you do, bring one with a low limit so you can't borrow more than you can afford to lose. Set your phone with a reminder, or even better, a series of reminders: Get up and walk around, have something to eat, enjoy the live entertainment, get ready to leave. Break up your time gambling by enjoying the other amenities and the tables or slot machines might not have quite the same hold on you when it's time to go. Partner up with someone to make sure you both leave in plenty of time to make it back to the ship. Create your own guardrails.

"You need to do this in life as well as in a casino. The lack of control encouraged by casinos is replicated everywhere. Stores and malls want you to engage in retail therapy, some financial advisors may want you to invest in potentially risky stocks or projects, con artists of all stripes will try to separate you from your money with the same thrilling feeling of rolling the dice. Maybe you want to limit your number of credit cards or the ceilings on them. Maybe you want to look into putting some assets into an irrevocable family trust. Freeze your credit so you'll need to call before you can open a new credit card or buy a new truck.

"Know your own weaknesses. Where are you likely to be financially irresponsible? Some people never gamble, but are easy prey for friends and family and sometimes even strangers who want to borrow money and never pay it back. Other people have no problem saying no to lending money, but can't resist a new gadget or set of golf clubs or even a new car. Knowing your weakness doesn't make you a bad person. We're all human, we all make mistakes. In fact, being willing to put steps in place to make it difficult—not impossible, just difficult enough to make you think twice or talk it over with someone else before you act—is a sign of strength."

William took a moment to look over his audience.

"The more you can put financial guardrails in place to protect yourself—from others and from your own impulses—the more you decide in advance just how much you are willing and able to lose, the more likely you are to come out of these encounters mostly unscathed.

"My mother had a system," William continued. "Some money from every paycheck went into each of three sugar bowls. The first sugar bowl was for emergencies, the second was to send her two kids to college, and the third sugar bowl was for her and my father's old age. The rest of the paycheck went to the essentials, and any left over from that could be used for fun. None of us dared to touch those sugar bowls; if Momma didn't think it was an emergency, we had to find some other way to raise whatever money we needed. This may sound draconian, but my mom built a future for our whole family out of those sugar bowls. You can do the same. Put some money where you can reach into it easily, but keep the rest where it will be safe from even your own worst decisions."

And with that, William put down his microphone and left the stage. Everyone in the audience was a little uncomfortable; no one could fail to think of financial mistakes they had made. Slowly, thoughtfully, they began to file out of the auditorium.

Reality Check: Shirley and Sam

While the rest of the passengers prepared for a shore excursion in Memphis, Shirley and Sam met up with Gunnar for their reality check. Shirley was nervous, but mostly she was grateful that they weren't meeting with William; he had been very stern in his lecture that morning.

"Rachael said William only seems intimidating," she told her husband as they headed for the ship's library, where Gunnar was holding his Reality Check meetings. "She promises that underneath it all, he's a sweetie."

"I'm sure he has a good side," Sam said, "only we didn't see it this morning. We saw the 'unhappy high school principal' side."

"He did make me feel as if I'd stayed out past curfew!" Shirley laughed. "I realize he had a point, but I'm still glad we're meeting with Gunnar."

Gunnar was waiting at the door to welcome them into his "office." Shirley was delighted with the floor-to-ceiling bookshelves filled with books ranging from nautical history to murder mysteries.

"How many of them have you read?" she asked.

"Not enough!" Gunnar looked around with a cheerful smile. "I sneak in a few pages between my sessions, and of course I have three going on my nightstand, but I still have a long way to go. I guess I'll just have to keep doing these cruises until I work my way through all of them."

"Shirley's a voracious reader," Sam told him. "I listen to audiobooks while I'm on the road, but Shirley goes through a stack a week. She keeps our local library in business."

"I like to learn new things," Shirley agreed. "Whether I'm reading fiction or nonfiction or even a magazine, I always pick up something new."

"I guess that's why we're here today," her husband added. "We're looking to pick up something new."

"That's a great reason," Gunnar agreed. He showed them to their seats and picked up his notepad. "Let's get started."

Gunnar had prepared a packet for each of them, including their answers to the questionnaire, some of the numbers he had come up with, and additional things to think about moving forward. He also left plenty of space for them to add information as they spoke.

Looking at it, Sam and Shirley both felt a moment of concern; it seemed so foreign to see their lives and futures totaled up in one column after another.

Gunnar seemed to sense their discomfort.

"Take a deep breath," he advised, "and remember you're not on trial here. You've done nothing morally wrong, no matter what the numbers are. You have always made the best possible choices in the moment; that's all any of us can do. We're just going to look at this snapshot of where you are now so you can make the best possible choices again, only this time for your future. Okay?"

Sam and Shirley nodded. It was time to look at the numbers.

Both Sam and Shirley are in their mid-fifties and work outside the home. Sam is a sales professional for a gift and novelty distributor. He has worked for three different distributors over his career. Although he has always worked primarily on commission and his current employer has no pension plan option, they do have a SIMPLE IRA plan, which is similar to a 401(k), and to which his employer contributes 2 percent of Sam's salary. Sam currently has about $80K in that plan.

Shirley started out working for her parents, and ultimately, when they were ready to retire, she bought out the family gift shop. She has contributed to an IRA for her entire working career, but when money was tight, she didn't max out her contributions. Her IRA currently has about $100K.

Both of their children are in college and Sam and Shirley are contributing toward tuition. Both their son and their daughter went to state colleges so they could graduate relatively free of student debt, but it still means that Shirley and Sam have been unable to put any extra money aside for retirement for the last several years.

Shirley makes $70K a year from running her business. Sam's income fluctuates, but with commissions and bonuses, he generally earns around $70K as well. In addition, they bought a small duplex when they were first married; although they have since bought a larger house, they have kept the duplex and rented it out. Sam travels a lot, so much of the maintenance and land-lord duties fall to Shirley, helped out by their children when they are home from college. The duplex doesn't make them much money, but the income from it does cover the mortgage, insurance, and property taxes. The few thousand dollars in profit the duplex generates brings their income up to about $150K per year. Also, they refinanced the duplex when they purchased the business from Shirley's parents and still have a $200K mortgage remaining, although the value of the duplex itself has increased to $400K.

Their current house was purchased at the top of the market, before the 2008 crash. They were underwater for a while, which had terrified Shirley, but Sam had reminded her that they had been planning to live there for the long haul in any case. The house has since regained its value and even appreciated a little, to $600K, but they still have a $350K mortgage on it. With Sam so often on the road, they have delayed many improvements to both their home and the duplex; both are showing signs of wear. Between checking accounts, savings accounts, and their emergency fund, they have about $100K in personal savings.

Gunnar smiled reassuringly. "I know this can be anxiety provoking. But you are both doing fine. You have a lot to work with, a lot of options, and that's a good place to be."

Shirley released a breath she didn't realize she'd been holding. "But our mortgages!" she exclaimed. "It sometimes keeps me up at night, thinking about how much we owe on the two houses. And there's so much upkeep we haven't done!"

Gunnar nodded. "That's a reasonable perspective. But you could also look at it this way: Both houses have appreciated beyond the mort-gage, so even if you had to sell them, you would come out ahead of the game. Also, you failed to take into account the value of your business. That value is twofold: There's the value of the actual inventory and fixtures, which I'm going to estimate at about $300K, and then there's the value of the business itself—you have a regular clientele, established vendors, trained workers. If someone were to buy the business from you, I think you would be able to get about $250K above the value of the inventory."

"I've never even thought about selling the business," Shirley admitted.

"Well, you're not doing it tomorrow," Gunnar said. "And maybe not even in ten years. But when Sam retires, you might want to cut back, maybe take on a partner? Or one of your children?"

Sam laughed. "Neither one of our kids wants anything to do with the business. My daughter is majoring in computer science and my son is an engineer who wants to design theme-park rides."

"Both sound like great careers," Gunnar said. He turned to Shirley. "How do you feel about the kids not wanting to take on the gift shop?"

"I'm delighted," Shirley said. "I never really felt as if I had a choice—I practically grew up helping my dad in the shop. And, to be fair, it was a great job for when the kids were little. My parents lived near the shop and my mom would watch them if they were home sick; I could always run by over lunch or if one of the kids needed me. But I'm happy that both of my children have found something they love to do for their careers."

Sam looked at his wife in surprise. "I never knew you felt that way."

Shirley shrugged. "You were on the road a lot. You still are. My parents and the staff at the shop, they were my safety net for a lot of years. And it's not as if I hate working there. I like the people I work with and I mostly enjoy chatting with customers, and, of course, meeting you there was a highlight of my life. But is selling stationery and fad dolls my passion? No, it's not."

Sam continued to look stunned, but Gunnar simply nodded. "What a lot of people don't realize is that careers are often a series of trade-offs between competing priorities. If you are drowning in student debt, you may have to take a higher-paying job even if it isn't in the field you really want to work in. Trying to raise kids while working can mean cutting back on hours or taking a job with less overtime or less travel, but also less money and less opportunity for advancement.

"You're at a moment in time where your kids are out of the house and you're envisioning what the next chapter of your life might be like. This is a great opportunity not just to make sure you're financially set, but also . . . how can I put this?" He paused for a second before resuming. "That you're creatively set, that you're personally fulfilled as well. It's a lot more than just toting up the numbers.

"Those are things for you to talk about together. Rachael is also great with guidance on how you might want to think about it. I'll just say that both you and Sam should consider not only how you're going manage financially, but also how you're going to thrive emotionally."

He turned to Sam. "It can be particularly hard on men who have done one type of job their entire adult lives. You may think you want to be free of the grind, but you may discover that a lot of your identity is tied up in that routine. You're good at your work, too, which means you get a lot of validation and status from it. You'll need to find something that doesn't just fill your time, but also provides you with the positive self-image that you now receive from your job.

"Now, having said all that, let us total up your numbers."

Gunnar turned his laptop so they could see the screen. "As I mentioned, you have several options when you retire. Shirley, you could sell your gift shop or you could continue part-time by leaning more on your staff, or you could bring on a partner and maintain an interest in the business while leaving the management to someone else. You could sell the duplex or continue renting it for a pretty reliable income."

"We could sell everything and move to Tahiti!" Sam joked.

Gunnar smiled. "That's always an option. I hear Tahiti is lovely. In fact . . . although I realize you probably don't mean that literally, you could actually sell everything and start fresh somewhere new. Almost anyone could benefit financially from downsizing to a smaller home or even an apartment in a more affordable area. For some, that would mean moving to a new state; for others, it might just be moving across town. But before making such a drastic change, you should be sure that the lifestyle matches the one you want to be living for the next thirty years."

"If you don't like cows, don't buy a dairy farm," Shirley quipped.

"That's it exactly," Gunnar agreed. "Some people enjoy a rural area with room to garden and old-time fishing holes. Other people would be bored with that in five minutes. If you enjoy theater or concerts, you don't want the only game in town to be the elementary school winter pageant. If the things you love to do are a couple of hours away, you will find yourself resenting your new life, and that is not a great way to live."

"Enjoy the journey," Shirley said. "That's what Rachael's been saying."

Gunnar nodded. "Even when I go over the numbers with you—with everyone—my job is to show you what your options are. Your job is to make decisions that give you a life you enjoy. Sometimes that means doing some creative thinking, coming up with a few out-of-the-box solutions. But it always starts with being honest with yourself about what it is you really love."

"What are some of our options?" Sam asked.

"As a matter of fact," Gunnar answered, "the first option is to sell everything—although I hadn't gone so far as to suggest moving to Tahiti." He nodded toward his laptop. "Here, let me show you the numbers."

AVAILABLE MONEY FOR INVESTMENT BY LIQUIDATING (AT CURRENT VALUES)

Duplex value	$400,000
Business value	$250,000
Store value	$300,000
TOTAL	**$950,000**

"Assuming a thirty-year retirement window and investing this money in a diverse portfolio, you could expect to draw an annual income from these savings each year over those thirty years," said Gunnar. "The amount you can withdraw each year for thirty years will depend on your rate of return. Also, since we used the current values of your assets, we are factoring into each of these numbers an inflation rate of 3 percent to cover projected growth.

"Retiring at fifty-five on just these assets—with the 3 percent rate of inflation—you would annually be able to withdraw the following," he said, drawing their attention back to his laptop.

INTEREST RATE ON $950,000	POTENTIAL ANNUAL WITHDRAWAL
6%	$48,468
8%	$61,798
10%	$76,557

"In addition to these funds," Gunnar told them, "you will be able to draw some money every year from your IRAs, and you still have your emergency fund and your home, but that 3 percent inflation rate will also impact how much everything costs you to buy: clothes, groceries, utilities. It also doesn't take into account health insurance expenses, since you won't be eligible for Medicare until your sixties, but at the same time, you would eventually be able to claim Social Security, which would give you a little boost. But, realistically, you are looking at a best-case scenario where you're living on a little over half of your current income."

Sam's breath came out in a whoosh. This was not what he'd been expecting to see. Shirley pointed to the $400,000 next to the duplex.

"What about our mortgage? We only have $200,000 equity in the duplex as it is."

"That's right," Gunnar agreed. "Part of my action plan for you, no matter which option you choose, is aggressively paying off that mortgage. Right now, you're using the income from the duplex for your own expenses; you probably also used it to build your emergency savings, which was a good choice. But at this point, you have $100K that you can tap into without penalty. You're in good shape, and should probably even consider investing maybe two-thirds of that in something that provides a safe and predictable rate of return. Even just making sure it's in a savings account that has a pretty good interest rate is a step up from keeping it in a checking account. You want to keep it fairly liquid without sacrificing all possibilities of growth.

"For the duplex, pumping its income into paying the mortgage off early would have tremendous benefits. In addition to giving you more equity, if you pay it off before you retire, it gives you a better cash flow when you'll need it the most.

"Paying off the duplex would be my top recommendation to you, no matter what option you choose. A second recommendation would be for you to stop deferring maintenance on both the duplex and your own home. Taking care of problems while they're still small is the difference between putting on a new roof—which is expensive—and putting on a new roof while also dealing with water damage to your walls and ceilings, which can be catastrophic.

"Also, keeping the duplex in top shape allows you to charge more for the rent, which in turn gives you money to 1) pay off the mortgage early and 2) charge market-rate rents. Too many people fail to take full advantage of rental properties; they just rent them and forget about them until the tenant either calls with a problem or moves on and they need to rent it again. But being on top of maintenance and maintaining curb appeal can increase the amount you can ask for a rental unit, while at the same time decreasing tenant turnover and enhancing property values.

"In fact, if you enjoy being a landlord, it's almost always better to invest in multiple units. For one thing, the cash flow is more predictable when you have multiple tenants at a property. You know you won't have every apartment filled all the time, but you'll never have them all empty at once. You're still only maintaining one physical property—one lawn, one roof—but the income possibilities are multiplied. Right now you have a duplex with two renters, but if property management is something you think you might want to consider, I would be keeping an eye open for a property with maybe six or eight units. Again, paying off the mortgage on the duplex would give you equity you could parlay into a down payment for a bigger investment."

"That would be a lot to take on," Shirley said doubtfully.

Sam, on the other hand, looked interested. "I've always felt we could do more with the place we already have. And you're right," he added, "I will need something to keep me busy whenever I retire. I'm used to being on the go; I get antsy when I take a week's vacation. Suddenly having nothing to do would drive me up the wall."

"It's not a decision you have to make right now," Gunnar said. "My suggestion that you start dedicating the rental income to pay down the mortgage stands, whether or not you decide to keep the property. Another question you want to ask yourselves is: Where would you want to live in retirement? There are things about your neighborhood—the quality of the local schools, for instance, or your commuting distance to work—that will no longer be important now that your kids are in college, or once you stop needing to commute.

"Your house might also be too big for just the two of you, or have too many stairs to manage as you get older. This is one of those changes that you need to be careful thinking about, though. Mindset matters. I don't like the term 'downsizing' because it signals a loss, a shrinking. Rather, think of it as maximizing the things you need to live the life you want and jettisoning the things you no longer need. Don't let decisions that worked for one phase of your life tie you down in the next phase. Take the time to think through your ideal lifestyle and start making decisions from the new life you want to lead."

"It looks like we'll have some time to think about it," Shirley said ruefully. "Given these numbers, I don't think we'll be retiring at fifty-five."

"Maybe not," Gunnar said. "Like with my friends Priyanka and Oliver, even a few extra years would give you more savings to lean on and a shorter wait for Social Security and Medicare to kick in. What I'd encourage you to do is start investing in yourselves, both by putting more money into your IRAs—max out your contributions if you can—and by investing time and energy into creating the things you want to do next. This is the time to lay the foundation for a side business or investment properties or a creative passion that will keep you feeling young even as you march into your eighties and beyond. Retirement may give you a chance to slow down, but that doesn't mean you can't remain active and engaged doing the things you love."

Shore Leave: Memphis

While Shirley and Sam were having their one-on-one session with Gunnar, the other couples took advantage of the shore excursions into Memphis. Betty and Joe headed for Graceland, the famous home of Elvis Presley.

Betty wanted to start by visiting his tomb. "It's only right that we pay our respects," she said. Joe held her hand as she got unexpectedly misty-eyed, remembering how they danced at their wedding to Elvis' "I Can't Help Falling in Love with You."

After that, they toured the house. Joe was surprised by how much fun it was to see where Elvis had actually lived, and he was impressed with the merging of a museum experience with the feeling that you were simply dropping in on an eccentric but very dear old friend. He and Betty ate hot dogs and drank soda in the Graceland cafeteria. They overheard one of the docents telling their tour group a story about Elvis and his cars.

"Word is," said the docent, "that Elvis developed such a relationship with a Cadillac dealer here in town that the man was always ready to bring Elvis a new car. Once, the dealer got a call at home at two in the morning: Elvis needed six new Cadillacs. He wanted to have them sent as gifts to six of his friends. I don't know for sure if the story is true, but I do know the Cadillac dealer would not have minded being woken up before dawn to sell six new cars!"

Betty and Joe smiled at the story and decided to take a peek at Elvis' collection of cars themselves before heading back to the ship. There was the red MG he drove in the movie *Blue Hawaii*, and of course his famous 1955 pink Cadillac. Joe really enjoyed the cars; Betty, on the other hand, looked thoughtful as they walked out.

"Not a Cadillac fan?" Joe asked her, smiling.

"If you want to get me a pink Cadillac," she answered tartly, "I won't say no." She stopped to look around at the mansion and the beautiful garden surrounding them. "No, it's just that I was thinking— all this stuff he collected. He never really got to enjoy it, did he? I mean, he was only forty-two when he died; that's more than ten years younger than we are now. It made me think about the money we spend on things we probably don't need. Do they make us happy?"

"It's not like we're out buying six Cadillacs every weekend!" Joe protested.

Betty swatted him on the arm. "I'm not saying we throw money away. And I'm not saying we should give up things we really love. All I'm suggesting is that maybe we think a little more before we buy something. Is it going to make our lives better? Or is it for other people to gawk at when they come to our home. Like, for instance, we've been talking about getting a new living room set, but do we need one? The one we have is very comfortable, it's just not as snazzy as we'd like. But is snazzy for us to enjoy or for us to impress our friends with when they visit? I just think there's something sad about having all of this stuff left behind when someone's life is over."

Joe took her hand. "I don't think we've lived our lives worrying about what other people think of us or our living room furniture," he told her. "But I understand your point. More stuff would never make us happier. I, for one, would prefer to spend our money on experiences like this trip, things that we can enjoy together and remember always."

Betty gave his hand a squeeze. "I'm glad we came to Graceland."

"Me, too," her husband answered. "But we'd better head back. I don't want tomorrow's lecture to be about nearly missing the boat again."

Just Starting Out

When Betty and Joe joined their friends at dinner, they discovered a new couple had joined the group.

"This is Maya and her husband, Andrei," Gabriela said, introducing them to the newcomers. "We met them on our Beale Street tour today."

Maya and Andrei were younger than the others, in their early thirties.

"My goodness!" Betty laughed. "You're starting to think of retirement early!"

Andrei shrugged. "It's more of a vacation than anything else. Maya's parents thought we needed a break from the kids, and her father is very into finance, so they sent us on this cruise."

"How lovely of them," Rose said. "How many children do you have?"

"Two," Maya replied. "The oldest is five and the little one is three. And while Andrei is here mainly to enjoy the view—"

"And the food!" he laughed.

"I'm excited to learn what we can do now to protect our future later," Maya said. "Although I will admit," she added, "I'm also thrilled to have some adult conversation for a change."

"And a break from cutting up other people's food, I bet!" Shirley teased.

"You have kids, too?" Maya asked.

"Yes, although by now they can both hold a knife and fork on their own," Shirley laughed.

"What do you two do?" Peter asked.

"I have a startup," Andrei said. "It's not glamorous, I'm afraid, but it is useful: anti-piracy software that can help other software companies protect their intellectual property."

"That does sound useful," Sam agreed. "What about you, Maya? Apart from the full-time job of raising rug rats!"

Everyone laughed. The couples with children remembered how exhausting it was when theirs were small.

"I will admit, I've had to put my career on the back burner since the youngest was born," Maya said. "I have a law degree and managed to pass the bar while I was pregnant with the first, but then she was born and I realized how much I loved being a mom. I really didn't want to miss those first years trying to hustle my way into the partnership track of a law firm somewhere."

"There's still a lot of balancing women have to do managing their careers and families," Rose said.

"I took the first shift while Andrei was building his business," Maya said. "But our daughter starts kindergarten in the fall and Andrei's now at a place where he can work from home a couple of days a week."

"So I'll be adding Mr. Mom to my résumé next month," Andrei

said. "Maya is starting part-time at a legal firm specializing in contract law."

"Congratulations!" Lamont said.

Maya smiled. "Thank you. It did seem like this was the perfect moment to start thinking about what we can put in place now that will make our lives easier in thirty or forty years."

"A long horizon makes a big difference," Peter said. "I wish we'd started thinking about retirement when we were your age."

Andrei shrugged. "The problem is, with a new business going and Maya picking up a little freelance work here and there, and even now only working part-time, not to mention two kids, we don't really have enough to start saving for retirement. I mean, I'm not knocking this cruise, but anything we learn here, it's going to be at least a few years before we can implement it."

"You never know," Gabriela said. "I would have thought the same thing with our situation even now, and we're a good few years ahead of you. But a lot of what we've learned so far makes sense to me. I think we'll be able to make some changes as soon as we get home."

"That, of course, is the real battle," said Sam. "It's great to learn what options are available, but it's a whole other thing to actually put in place changes that will pay off in ten or twenty years."

He and Shirley told the group about their meeting with Gunnar.

"On one hand," Shirley said, "I'm relieved. I really didn't think we were even in the ballgame. On the other hand, I feel like a dope for not having thought about what we would do, how we would actually live, after retirement."

"It's interesting that Gunnar isn't taking Social Security into account," Joe mentioned. "Don't a lot of people rely on Social Security income once they retire?"

"Sure, they count on it," Lamont said. "But that's probably a mistake. Even if you delay taking it until you get full benefits—and that's, what, waiting until you're seventy?—it's never going to be enough to match your pre-retirement income."

"That's a good point," Rose said. "My mother ended up having to move in with my sister after my father died. I know my sister appreciated having her there, especially when her kids were small. But I know there were times when my mother regretted not being able to afford a place of her own."

"I would feel cheated, I think," said Betty thoughtfully, "if I'd worked hard all my life and at the end of it, there was only enough money to survive. Not to travel or have the freedom to enjoy life."

"The worst thing is," her husband pointed out, "that we would be the ones having cheated ourselves."

As dinner wrapped up, Rose looked around the table and smiled.

"Let's not end the evening on a down note," she said. "We all have some homework to do, and maybe some hard thinking about how we want to live our lives. But I, for one, am taking Rachael's advice to enjoy the journey. Who wants to join me in the piano bar?"

Thanks to Rose's good nature and common sense, the evening ended on a positive note as the couples got to know each other better while listening to a wonderful singer in the piano bar. But as they went back to their rooms, Shirley and Sam remained thoughtful, each one thinking about how they might want to reconsider their assumptions about retirement and instead build a more deliberate—and enjoyable—future.

Chapter Four

CYCLES

The Morning Ritual

The men once again met up to walk a few laps and greet the day. Andrei had already been up and jogging; when he saw the men, they invited him to cool down by walking a couple of laps with them. He trotted over and they walked in silence for a few moments, enjoying the fresh air.

"I wonder what today's lesson will be," said Peter.

"So long as it's not another dressing-down, I'm in," Andrei said. "I didn't like it when people lectured me in high school—I'm sure not going to pay good money to have someone treat me like a child now."

"How much did you lose at the casino?" joked Joe.

"That's not the point," Andrei insisted.

Sam and Lamont shared a look.

"Two hundred?" Lamont whispered.

"At least," Sam replied.

"I am an adult," Andrei said pointedly. "And gambling is entertainment. I don't argue with someone who wants to go to a fancy restaurant and spend a couple of hundred on dinner and wine when they could get the same calories from a food truck and have the same amount of fun at a cheap happy hour. If I want to spend that money enjoying my time in a casino, why should that be morally wrong?"

"I don't think it was gambling itself that William was objecting to," Lamont countered. "I think it was how quickly people got hooked. You need to put some serious safeguards in if, after just an hour or two, you're willing to miss your boat to play one more hand."

Sam shrugged. "Casinos do whatever they can to make gambling enticing. All those bells and whistles create hits of dopamine that make it hard to stop."

"So do video games," Andrei said. "In some sense, so does anything enjoyable. But people are able to put down their crossword puzzles or their gaming consoles and go on about their day. I don't understand why he went ballistic over casino gambling—a stop, we should remember, the cruise made on purpose."

"Do you think it was a test?" Joe asked.

"Not a test so much as a setup," Andrei replied. "He knew some people wouldn't want to leave and so he had his lecture already prepared. Those of us who can handle gambling without mortgaging the house were forced to sit through it."

Peter looked thoughtful. "Do we know, though, if we really can handle gambling?" he asked. "I have a friend who's a great guy, a smart guy, and he ended up losing everything, including his marriage, because he couldn't stop gambling. We've been friends since our thirties and I never would have guessed that he would put his whole life, and his kids' lives, on the line like that."

"Maybe that was the point of the lecture," Lamont said. "Give some people a chance to recognize themselves and take stock before they do something irrevocable."

"What's interesting to me," Joe added, "is that it can be hard to tell if you're gambling or investing. I mean, sure, spinning a roulette wheel is clearly gambling. You have no control over whether your number will come up or not. But the same can be true of the stock market. You don't really have a say in how a company runs or what the economy is doing that might trigger a massive downturn in the market."

"True," Sam agreed, "but at least there's something there behind your money—a physical thing being produced or a service provided.

With gambling, you're not buying anything other than the thrill of the moment. Whether you have more money or less money at the end of a session at the slot machines or a spin of the roulette wheel, there's nothing physical to back that up. You're not investing in something that could have long-term success—it's all short term, in the moment."

"Which is why I compared it to a dinner out," said Andrei. "Or going to see a movie—or, I guess, if we're trying to use comparable amounts of money, taking some friends to a Broadway play. What you get is the experience."

"What I think is ironic," Peter added, "is that gambling is legal only when the government gets a cut. State-sanctioned gambling is considered moral, but gambling where they're not collecting revenue from it? That's somehow immoral."

"I don't really like to gamble," said Lamont. "It's not that I'm immune to the rush of winning, and Gaby and I had a good time hanging out at the casino the other night. But I can't open my wallet too far without remembering that the house always wins. My cousin," he explained, "is a croupier at a casino. He told me all the games have their odds set in favor of the house. Even when you think your skill plays a part, like in blackjack, for instance, the odds are tipped slightly in favor of the house. Over the long term, the casino will always win—which means you will always lose. Gaby and I decided ahead of time how much we were willing to part with, and I think we've maybe been in three casinos in our whole lives. One of them was where my cousin works, and that was probably the most fun, because we got a little bit of an insider's view of it." Lamont grinned. "Plus, they comped our rooms!"

Sam nodded. "I really think you have something there. Whether we're talking about a casino visit or putting money in stocks or even investing in your own business, it's important to plan out ahead of time how much you're willing to lose. How much you can afford to lose. And then have some support in place so that when you have to, you can pull the plug and actually get out."

"It's good to decide to leave while you're up as well," Peter added. "Both in the casino and in the stock market. I think people believe that what goes up will always go up, but markets turn and luck runs out. Deciding to quit while you're ahead, rather than keep playing until you're down, that's a game changer. At the very least, recoup the money you invested, maybe with a little more, and then keep playing with your winnings. But maybe," he shrugged, "I'm thinking about this more lately because Rose and I have already retired. We can't afford to wait out a recession—we need money we can tap into without being forced to sell at the bottom of the market."

"This cruise is making me look at our finances in a whole new way," Joe said. "And it's only Day Four!"

LECTURE 3: CYCLES

After breakfast, the group met up in the auditorium. Slides projected onto a screen onstage let them know that William's theme today was "Cycles."

"From time immemorial," William began, "there have been cycles of feast and famine in the natural world. We should expect nothing less from the financial world.

"First, there was hunting and gathering. People were dependent on the local food supply, and if that migrated or was ruined by a cold snap or a drought, the choices were to migrate ourselves in search of a new food source or die of hunger. Not a lot of options were available.

"Luck played a part, but then eventually so did agriculture: the deliberate planning and creation of a food supply. Hopefully a diverse one that could withstand the vicissitudes of weather, pests, and disease. Even today, farmers are constantly dealing with events over which they have no control, while at the same time trying to control as much of the growing process as they can. But one of the reasons our food supply is so robust in the United States is that we are able to import food from around the world. Your daily breakfast banana, for instance, is dependent upon our access to food from other countries and climates. Not every country is able to import food or have the infrastructure to distribute it in an emergency. We are still, as human beings, subject to nature's cycles for some of our most basic needs.

"Why am I lingering on avocados and grapes? Because trade developed as people began bartering with their surpluses. Farmers bartered with other farmers, villages with other villages. The biggest stumbling block back then was: How much is a bushel of apples worth in eggs or milk or zucchini? Negotiation was baked into bartering—if you'll forgive the pun—because there was no agreed-upon basis for exchange.

"As civilization developed, production of goods and services came into being, and then we were really facing a dilemma. If I help you shoe your horse, are you going to pay me in oats or carrots or in time, helping me dig my well? Things like barn-building in the Old West were community events because at some point everyone was going to need many hands to help them build a house or a barn or a forge. The exchange was implicit: You help me now and I'll help you later. I'm sure there were similar arrangements in villages all over the world, because one of the things we needed to do to survive as a species was rely on each other."

As he was talking, William clicked through slides showing different cultures over the course of centuries working together, farming, and bartering.

"At some point, however," he continued, "bartering or even the implicit contract of 'you-wash-my-back-and-I'll-wash-yours' broke down. Life became too complex for simple barters to handle. And so people, ever resourceful, developed a medium of exchange. First, things like shells and beads, and then eventually, gold, coins, and paper money.

"But even the most modern forms of currency and digital banking, while infinitely more flexible than tomatoes or goats, are still not perfect. We still have cycles. They may not be feast and famine—although, across the world, we still do have those things—but they are financial cycles of depression, recession, and inflation.

"Over the next few days I'm going to go deeper into cycles and what we can do about them, but for now, suffice it to say that in periods of depression, values of goods and services are severely *depressed*—that is, nothing is worth as much anymore. This often includes the very things people depend upon as they start thinking about retirement, like the value of their house, which they might have planned to sell. In depressions, workers often lose their jobs as businesses retrench or even go bankrupt. An investor's financial worth can drop dramatically. The most well-known of these depressions is, of course, the Great Depression of 1929.

"A recession is a milder form of depression. The economy declines, businesses contract. Generally, recessions are sparked by consumers spending less money, but of course there are many reasons for that. If, for whatever reason, a recession occurs and people lose their jobs, they have less money to spend, and that can become a vicious cycle whereby they then spend even less. You can see how what might start as a temporary recession could spiral down into something much more significant and long-lasting.

"Both recessions and depressions can happen when the economy slows down, but what happens when an economy heats up? One of the ways the government combats recessions and depressions is by increasing the money supply, but that in turn can lead to inflation. Inflation means that goods and services start to cost more, and so your dollar—or worse, your future dollar—is worth less. Slow and steady inflation: not bad. Hyperinflation: disastrous.

"Stagflation is yet another possibility. This is a period of slow growth and high unemployment coupled with high inflation. This is a doozy of a problem for economists, because tackling inflation with their usual toolbox could slow the economy even further and exacerbate unemployment. We think economists know what to do, but to some extent, we're all still just trying to control the elements.

"These cycles are unpredictable and not something to be solved by any individual investor, but that doesn't mean you can't plan for them and hedge your bets. This is why you hear people talk constantly about having a diversified portfolio, which at heart just means to not put all your eggs in one basket. Having your money in different kinds of investments gives you options. It allows you to be nimble when things go awry. Which they will.

"But we'll talk more about that in the coming days. For today, let the idea of cycles start to take hold. You can't control them, but you can learn to ride them out. The only real danger lies in putting your head in the sand and hoping they won't happen. So think about that and, as always, enjoy the journey!"

Shore Leave: Greenville

The couples were excited to disembark for a tour of Greenville, Mississippi. There were so many museums and places of interest that most of the couples set off on their own and agreed to meet back at the ship for a late lunch.

Peter and Rose went with Lamont and Gabriela to an exhibition of vintage cars.

"Form and function!" Lamont looked with satisfaction at the cars on display. "This speaks to my heart as a graphic designer."

"It speaks to my heart because I remember when a lot of these cars were on the road," Peter laughed. "One of the first cars I remember knowing the name of was that 1950 Chevrolet Bel Air. And I remember my grandfather had one of these Buicks from the 1930s—it was old even when I was a kid!"

"Your grandfather should have hung onto that car," his wife teased. "It's a collectible now, a valuable antique—like me!"

Peter smiled at her tenderly. "You are not an antique," he told Rose. "You are a treasure. And I'm glad he didn't keep the car. Yes, they're worth a lot today, but not in the condition he kept that old thing in. He drove it into the ground."

"That's why the cars are worth so much," Gabriela said. "So few of them were kept in good condition. People owned them because they needed to get around, not because they were investing in a collectible. It's not like laying down port."

"I'm sorry," said her husband. "What is 'laying down port,'? and how do you even know about it?"

"Some of us like words, not just pictures," she teased him. "The mystery writer Dorothy L. Sayers had her hero, Lord Peter Wimsey, lay down port when his son was born," Gabriela explained. "The idea is that you buy a case of good port—a vintage year—when your child is born and put it in your wine cellar. Then you don't touch it for a couple of decades, and by the time your son is of drinking age, the port has not only aged appropriately, but might also be worth a lot more than you paid for it."

"Oh, now you make me wish we'd done that for our boys!" Rose exclaimed. "What a romantic idea."

"It just runs into a bit of a snag these days," Peter remarked, "when most people don't have a wine cellar."

Gabriela laughed. "That's right! I actually looked into it on a whim when we were married, and the only option would have been to pay a wine store to house the port for us—you can't just stick it in the garage; it has to be temperature controlled. And while I am a romantic, I'm also a businesswoman. Any gain we might have made selling the port on our twenty-fifth anniversary would have been greatly lessened by what it would have cost just to store it for twenty-five years."

"Well, I think it's very romantic that you were willing to bet we'd still be together in twenty-five years," Lamont said, giving her hand a squeeze. "Points to you for looking into it."

"There is something magnetic about the idea that you can just keep something long enough that it becomes valuable to someone else," mused Rose. "I suppose the trick is to know what."

"And the danger," said Peter, "is to assume everything will have value eventually. It's just not true. Some fads will burn out, other things you'd never think of will rise in value only to fall again. People used to go nuts for things like McDonald's toys or Pez dispensers, but you could have a box full of them now and they wouldn't be worth what you paid for them. The same is true of stamps, much to my disappointment. I started my stamp collection as a boy, but it's not really worth anything now."

"Except in the pleasure it gave you to collect them," Rose reminded him.

"That should always be the deciding factor," agreed Gabriela. "If you enjoy doing something, like collecting stamps or baseball cards—or, I guess these days, if my nieces and nephews are any indication, Pokémon cards—keep at it. Just don't assume that's how you'll fund your retirement. Even if everyone else is doing it."

"That's pretty much the definition of a fad, isn't it? A mass of people all going after the same thing?" Lamont said. "As an artist, I'm looking at the NFT world where that's exactly what's happening and I'm wondering how I can get in on it before it completely collapses."

"I don't even know what an NFT is," admitted Peter.

"It's an acronym for the ridiculous name of 'non-fungible token,'" explained Lamont. "People are paying money, tens and hundreds and sometimes millions of dollars, for the bragging rights of owning a digital piece of art."

"You mean they can't even put it on their wall?" exclaimed Rose.

"Not a real wall in the real world," said Lamont. "There are virtual walls in virtual galleries where you can hang your digital art."

"And people pay money for this?" Peter asked, incredulous.

"The most expensive one I know of was auctioned off for over $69 million," Lamont told him.

"That's an enormous amount of money!" Rose exclaimed.

"Which is why I would love to have some of my art go for that," Lamont laughed.

"When you're at that level, though," Peter said, "it's not really about the art, is it? I mean, once collectibles are worth that much money, we amateur collectors are out of the mix. It's all professionals looking for places to store their money."

"And to one-up each other," Gabriela said.

"Which makes them vulnerable to con artists and frauds," Lamont added. "This happens all the time in the art world. Even museums get caught up in it, wanting to believe that something is real because it would be such a coup for their collection. Con artists prey on people's desire to have what no one else has."

"Even when that thing is virtual," Peter said shrewdly.

"Even then," Lamont agreed. "Personally, I don't think virtual art can sustain its value. I may be wrong, though. A lot of people are putting a lot of money into it."

"Gambling a lot of money, you mean," said Rose.

"That takes us back to investing first of all in things you love," said Gabriela. "If you collect things for fun or because you love them or believe them to be beautiful, then if they end up being worth money someday, that's a bonus."

The couples walked on for a while longer, looking at the vintage cars, until Rose began to tire. They headed over to a hotel that offered afternoon tea, and the conversation turned to scones and favorite hotels where they had stayed. Then Rose circled back to one of their earlier conversations.

"I do think being financially ready for retirement is important," she said, "but I also think it's important to enjoy the journey. No one knows how much time they have left. If you spend it hoarding your money for a future you may not have, you'll never get to enjoy meeting new friends and having a lovely day with them, as we've just had with you."

Gabriela raised her cup of tea. "To new friends," she said.

Everyone raised their cups for the toast. "New friends," they chorused.

Reality Check: Joe and Betty

While everyone else had been getting ready for their shore excursion to Greenville, Betty and Joe had headed to Gunnar's office for their Reality Check. After talking to Sam and Shirley the night before, they were excited to learn what they could do to start their own retirement on solid ground.

Gunnar rose to meet them.

"Welcome to my lair," he said. "Not as scenic as Greenville, but I hope just as exciting."

"For us, it sure is," Joe said. "Betty and I feel like we're poised on the next big adventure, and you're the one who's going to push us off into it."

"So long as it's not off a cliff!" Betty said. "I admit, I'm a little more nervous about it than Joe is."

"No need to be nervous," Gunnar told them. "My job is to show you that you have more options than you think you do. Then it'll be up to you to make the adventure happen. To get started, why don't you tell me a little bit about yourselves?"

"Betty and I have been sweethearts since high school," Joe answered. "I really want for both of us to enjoy our lives together once the heavy lifting of working and raising kids is behind us."

"Joe joined the army right after high school," Betty said. "I went to college and got a B.A. in education and almost right away started teaching. I took a couple of years off when the boys were little, but I have twenty-six years in the classroom under my belt at this point."

"And how much longer do you want to keep working?" Gunnar asked.

"That depends if you're asking me on the first day of school or the last!" Betty replied with a laugh. "I do enjoy teaching, but it can be all-consuming. I teach high school English, and there's a good bit of pressure on the kids to do well on all the standardized tests that can help them get into college. Which means there's a lot of pressure on the teachers to teach to the test. That part's not so fun. It's hard to help kids develop a love of the language and of literature when you're trying to cram in everything that might or might not appear on a standardized test. I like to joke that I have a couple of good years left in me, and maybe three mediocre ones after that."

"Me, I'm ready to retire now," Joe said. "Our boys are both out of college and self-sufficient, and I've been working for the same machine shop for thirty-four years. There's constant pressure for more and more production. I feel like they forget that the people who work there are people, not machinery ourselves." Joe looked a little abashed. "In fact, I've already let them know I plan to retire soon. That's how we found out about this cruise, through H.R. So if it turns out I need to work for another ten years, we may be in trouble."

Gunnar smiled. "I'm never going to tell you that you have to do this or you must do that," he said. "My goal is to show you which options are available. If continuing to work at the machine shop is off the table—either because you've already given notice or because you just don't want to work there anymore—that's not a problem. There are always other options. Let's take a look."

Joe, sixty-one, and Betty, sixty, have a joint savings and checking account totaling $95,000.

They own their home outright; it's worth $300,000.

Joe's pension: $45,000
Betty's pension: $55,000
Total pension (annual income): $100,000

If they sell their home and invest that income with their savings, and assuming 3 percent inflation, they could anticipate being able to take out:

INTEREST ON $395,000 FOR 30 YEARS	POTENTIAL ANNUAL WITHDRAWAL
6%	$20,152
8%	$25,695
10%	$31,831

Assuming a mid-level average return of 8 percent per year, they would be able to withdraw $25,695 per year for thirty years from their investment portfolio, giving them a total annual income of just over $125,000.

An investment in a Standard & Poor's 300 account and a Russell 2000 investment account historically average around 10 percent. These are two investment accounts that do well over the long term, and built into these accounts is ample diversification.

"Here's the most important thing I want you to see," Gunnar told them. "By keeping your savings in your bank account, you are actually losing money," he said. "I know, it's liquid and easy to access, but the interest rate is miniscule. That same amount in a diversified stock portfolio or index fund would get you several times the return on investment. It's important to have some money that is easily accessed in case of emergency, but it's just as important to make your money work for you."

"Risk versus reward," Joe said.

"Exactly that," Gunnar agreed. "What people don't always understand is that a no-risk investment still has a risk attached to it: the risk that your money will be worth less and less as time goes on. Inflation is something you have to take into account. If your money isn't at least keeping pace with that, you will eventually find yourself in a squeeze."

"What about our home?" Betty said, focusing on the one thing Gunnar had mentioned that really had her concerned. "I don't think I want to sell my home."

"And you don't have to," Gunnar assured her. "It's one option. You would have to live somewhere, and for some people after retirement, it makes sense to find a smaller place that better meets your needs. Some people want to move closer to their children. Some people, as they get older, like renting because it means that someone else is responsible for fixing leaks, for instance. The game changer is remembering that everything is on the table."

"I see how that could be exciting," Betty said, "but it can also be a bit overwhelming."

"Have you talked at all about how you each envision retirement?" Gunnar asked.

Their blank looks told him all he needed to know.

"Again," he said gently, "I'm not trying to force you into any decision. But it is in your best interest to think these things through. Joe, what do you do with your time now, when you're not at work?"

"Well, I'm with Betty," Joe answered. "And I volunteer once a week at the veterans hospital, but mostly I putter around the house. I do like to fix things. I've put thirty years into making our house really fit our dreams. I built out a sunroom and a porch. I finished the attic. I turned the basement into a workroom. That house really suits us and I'd regret having to leave it now that we might have some time to enjoy it."

Gunnar smiled. "It sounds like the house is something you both want to continue to live in. That's great! The first step is figuring out what you want—and hopefully, as with the house, you'll find you both want the same thing."

He went over the numbers with them again. "With just your pensions, you'll have $100K per year to live on. That's less than with both of you working full-time, but let's see how much less it would really be.

"Both of you have over two decades each in good jobs with benefits. Joe, you're currently making $70K a year, and Betty, you're making $72K. So $100K a year is just over two-thirds of your current income. But let's not panic.

"First of all, Betty is not ready to retire. That means that for the next few years—let's say five—Betty will still be bringing in $72K, maybe a little more. Joe, your pension is $45K, so together, that's $117K—a little less than you're currently making, but still over $100K. You'll also still have health insurance coverage through Betty's employer, so you won't have to worry about that extra cost.

"Here's what I want you to do: I want you to actually live on $100K for the next five years. I want you to automatically deduct some money from each paycheck so that you're putting $17K a year into an investment account like the ones I mentioned.

"This helps you in two ways. First, it lets you see what it'll be like living on $100K a year. Is this, in fact, the way you want to live, or would you rather travel more or move somewhere else? Getting a taste of it while you still have other options is a good way to start deciding what really matters to you. There will always be things that would be nice to have, mind you—I would love to spend six months a year traveling the world, but I have competing priorities, like wanting my kids to grow up near my parents. Having a test run, if you will, gives you a chance to sort out whatever your competing priorities might be.

"The second thing this does is help build your investments for the future. Investing $17K a year for five years gives you $85K, and that's before counting in the amount that money will appreciate as stocks rise and dividends are added to the principal. In five years, you will have matched the $95K that, right now, represents what you've saved in your last thirty years together."

"That's incredible!" Betty gasped.

Gunnar shrugged. "People vastly underestimate the value of putting a little money aside every month," he said. "If you had started just by investing a little more every time you got a raise, you wouldn't have noticed a change in your standard of living, but you'd be much more secure financially now. On the other hand, you do have a safety net in that you both have jobs with pensions. A lot of people nowadays have to set money aside in things like IRAs because so many jobs no longer have pensions, and even if they do, people's careers are so much more fluid than they used to be."

"I had to be careful," Betty admitted, "when I took time off each time my children were born. I took sabbaticals rather than quitting and coming back to work later—that way, I didn't lose my seniority and I could be sure to be vested in my pension. But it was a sacrifice. I would much rather have stayed home with the boys."

"There are so many trade-offs we never really think about until we're faced with them," Gunnar agreed. "The same is going to be true in retirement."

"Better to get a taste of them before we're committed," Joe said.

"That's it exactly," said Gunnar.

"What happens if we discover we don't want to live on only $100K a year?" Betty asked.

Gunnar smiled. "Then you have some other options."

"I'm still not going to want to sell my home." Joe looked mulish.

"That's fine," Gunnar said, "but how about renting out a room?"

"A room? Like a boarding house?" Joe asked.

"Not quite," Gunnar said. "But you do have the boys' room empty now, right?"

Betty nodded. "We have two empty bedrooms. When the boys got older, Joe finished the attic and our oldest son moved up there."

"You live in a college town," Gunnar reminded them. "What about renting those two rooms to a couple of undergraduates? Or even just the attic room? Renting those during the school year only would be a boon to kids who usually have to sign a year's lease, even if they only live there for nine or ten months. And you could make an extra $15K a year or more, depending on local rent prices and how many rooms you decided to let. Again, if you invested that money for a few years instead of spending it, you'd have more of a nest egg when you finally decide you'd prefer to be alone.

"Also," he said, turning to Joe, "I think you should consider part-time work. Not just for the money, or even primarily for it, but because you're used to having a sense of mastery in your work. The real shock to the system when you retire is that you lose that space where you shine, where you are acknowledged as being a valuable part of a team.

"It sounds to me," Gunnar continued, "as if you have a real gift for building things with your hands. Remodeling, building a porch. You might consider anything from local handyman jobs to creating handmade furniture. The key here is to find something you love to do and match it with something people need done. Either one without the other is doomed to fail, especially as a side business in your retirement. You don't want to be spending your time doing something you dislike—"

"Heck," said Joe, "I could go back to work if I wanted to do that."

"Exactly!" Gunnar laughed. "But you also don't want to spend a lot of time marketing or, even worse, hustling for clients. Think about what kinds of things people already ask you to do. You probably give your time and talent freely to your friends, and I'm not saying you should stop doing that. What I'm saying is to get some business cards printed and start asking your friends to pass them out to their friends, along with a mention of your reasonable rates. There's no reason for you not to be paid for something you enjoy and do well."

"And it'll keep him off the streets," Betty laughed.

"That's true," Joe said. "We used to say that about our boys all the time, and I'd pull them into helping with my projects in the workshop. What was true for them is also true for me—having something to do keeps you from wandering around aimlessly and getting into trouble."

"And the trouble a lot of men get into," Gunnar added, "is social isolation and a lack of purpose. Both of those can shorten your life, and we don't want that. That is the opposite of enjoying your golden years."

"Well," Betty said, "you have certainly given us a lot to think about. I'm glad we have options."

"And a bit of a runway," Gunnar added. "Despite Joe turning in his notice already."

"Maybe I'll tell them I'll stick around to the end of the year," Joe said thoughtfully. "At least until I get my business cards made up."

My Cup of Tea

After the Reality Check, Betty decided to have tea in the lounge while Joe took a nap. She met Maya and Shirley there.

"Where's Sam?" Betty asked.

"He saw the putting green was empty, with so many people still ashore, and was off like a shot!" Shirley laughed. "Me, I was going to sit and relax my tired feet. We must've walked miles this morning."

"Every place we've stopped has been more interesting than the last," Maya said. "There's so much to see."

"I'm glad you're having a nice time," Betty said. "You must miss your kids."

"Absolutely," Maya agreed. "On the other hand, I'm enjoying getting to sleep through the night for a change! I'm not quite sure what I'm going to do when I go back into the workforce."

"There are so many things women need to juggle," Shirley said.

"That sounds like my cue," said a voice behind her.

The women looked up to see Rachael helping herself to a cup of tea. "May I join you?" she asked.

Shirley made space for her on the banquette. "What lessons have you for us today?" she asked.

Rachael laughed. "I'm more of a question answerer than a lecturer. But the idea that women have a lot to juggle is one that's near to my heart."

"I have a question about that," said Maya. "I wasn't joking when I said I wasn't sure what I would do going back into the workforce. The kids are still little and need a lot of time and attention. Andrei will be taking them to preschool and kindergarten and picking them up two days a week while he works from home. I'm on mom duty two days a week and in the office for three, so my mom will step in on Fridays, when both Andrei and I are needed at work. I can see how any little unexpected thing could throw our whole lives into a tizzy. I guess my question is: What do I do?"

Maya looked a little sheepish asking such a broad question, but Rachael smiled reassuringly.

"Thank you for asking such a great question," she said. "That's actually the real question all of us want answered—about everything. 'What do I do? What actions can I take to protect myself, to keep it all from falling down around me?' William is going to tackle some of that when he talks about recessions later today—you can think of that as a macro version of the same question: What do we do when something goes wrong?

"And the answer is that you assume things will go wrong and plan for them ahead of time.

"I'll leave the macro answers for William, but I'd love to talk about your specifics and some of the special issues facing women in general. First, to your point, you have designed a very sophisticated solution to a specific problem, which is who will pick up your children from school. You have problem-solved and I congratulate you. You have also noticed that this solution only works if all the pieces work exactly as planned, and you're smart enough to know that in life, this is rarely the case. So what do you do?

"Start by assuming the worst. Let's say that someone gets sick or an emergency comes up and that neither your husband nor your mother can pick up the kids. What then?"

"I'd take off from work and go get them," Maya replied promptly.

"Of course you would. And as a short-term Band-Aid, that's a viable solution. But what if it happens again? Or what if one care-giver—either your mother or your husband—fell out of rotation for a week or more? The longer the problem continues, the less viable your solution becomes.

"This is true of everything. Everything! You need to have a safety net with multiple layers in place to ensure a soft landing. In your case, I would start by meeting other parents in both the school and the preschool and see who you really like, who parents the same way you do. When you make friends who have the same problems to solve, you can often help each other—in this case, by agreeing to swap emergency playdates whenever necessary.

"You should also have a frank talk with your husband about what happens when something comes up at your work and you can't pick up the kids on one of your caregiving days. What kind of notice would he need to be able to rearrange his schedule? I know he runs his own business, but that doesn't mean he is in complete control of his calendar—there will always be clients to meet with or employees to supervise.

"You should have a similar conversation with your mother. Do you have a babysitter you like? Maybe a college student who might also have a flexible schedule?

"You want to have enough options that what you considered your first option—to leave work early—actually becomes your last. It is by far the most expensive option because, rightly or wrongly, it can lower your perceived value in the eyes of your employers. A lot of companies will talk about the importance of putting family first, but when they see you actually do it, that's a different matter. Even your husband taking off early because of a childcare issue is less of a problem because he runs his own business. No one is looking over his shoulder or clocking his hours."

"That was such a relief for me when my kids were little," Shirley said. "Sure, I had the gift shop to run, but for a long time, my boss was my mother and she loved having the kids there. We set up a play area for when they were really tiny, and later they used it when one of them wasn't feeling well enough to go to school. And then when I ran the store, I let my assistants use it for their children. Not a month went by when we didn't have a few days with a little one underfoot."

Maya looked aghast. "Oh, my gosh!" she said. "I didn't even think about what to do if they got sick! And of course they will. I was just thinking about picking them up after school!"

"It's the same type of problem with many of the same solutions," Rachael reassured her. "Shirley, thank you so much for your input! Maybe you and Betty could help Maya brainstorm all the things that can go wrong? And share some of your own solutions?"

"I'd love that!" said Maya.

"You three have stumbled across one of the most important and least used resources you will ever have," Rachael told them. "Your network. The people you know, and especially those who have already gone through whatever you're facing now. They have perspective, they have solutions, and they know what unforeseen problems might be lurking around the corner. Tapping into your network for advice and support is one of the smartest steps you can take, whether you're building a safety net for childcare or starting a business or planning your retirement. You can get a glimpse of the future by asking advice from people who are further along on their journey than you are.

"And look," Rachael continued, "I don't want to scare you, but it would be malpractice not to make sure you know how different financial pictures can be for women than for men. Women live longer, so their savings have to last longer. Also, because they live to an older age, they may have more health-related costs, including caregivers or nursing home expenses. You need to factor those things in and not just base your retirement on your husband. And don't get me started on divorce!"

"I have friends who have gotten divorced," Betty said, "and while it was the right decision for them, some of them were completely blindsided by money matters."

"Divorce leaves men relatively unscathed financially," Rachael agreed, "whereas it can plunge women into poverty. And not just women with young children. According to the Government Accountability Office, for women over 50, divorce means your household income will fall an average of 41 percent—that's the average, which means for some women, it's a lot worse. For men, that same divorce causes half as much financial damage. And it can wreak havoc with your retirement plan: There's still a pay gap for women, which makes it even harder to climb back up the ladder when you only have your own paycheck to count on. And let's not forget that many women, like Maya, put their own careers on hold when their children are born, putting them several years behind comparable men.

"These are all things you need to consider when you're putting together your retirement plan. Don't panic, but don't pretend none of this affects you. Knowing what can go wrong gives you the power to plan for it. And the peace of mind that comes with knowing you'll be fine no matter what goes wrong? That is priceless."

Dinner: The Emerald Isle

All five couples met up at dinner. Chef Luigi had chosen an Irish theme, with baked potatoes, lamb stew, and corned beef.

The couples quickly found themselves comparing notes. Maya, Betty, and Shirley shared what they had learned from Rachael, particularly the idea of brainstorming all the things that can go wrong instead of putting your head in the sand and hoping everything will be perfect. Sam and Betty offered to share their lecture notes with everyone.

"I'll start a document on Google Drive," Betty said. "Then we'll all have access and everyone can add to it."

"You might need to talk me through that," Peter laughed. "I'll get there in the end, mind you, but I'm on the other side of the computer revolution."

"Chalk it up to another new thing learned on this trip," his wife told him. "Although I have to say, the whole idea of recessions is upsetting."

"You should have been at tea with us," Maya told her. "We ended up brainstorming everything that could go wrong once the kids go to school next month. One disaster after another!"

"If you want to talk about disasters," said Joe, "look no further than the Irish stew." He speared a bit of potato. "The Irish Potato Famine caused enormous death and misery. About a million people died of starvation out of a population of just over 8 million. More than one in ten!"

"That ties into what Rachael was saying earlier," Shirley added. "You need to have multiple solutions available to be able to bounce back. I may be wrong, but didn't the Irish over-rely on just the one crop, potatoes?"

"It was even worse than that," Lamont said. "They relied on only a couple of high-yielding types of potatoes. So the genetic diversity wasn't even there. When a—What was it, a fungus? Mold?—attacked the potatoes, they didn't have another type of potato that was maybe more resistant to attack to fall back on. And it spread across the entire country."

Betty nodded. "People were doing what they thought best in the moment. Most of the poor got as much as 80 percent of their calories from potatoes and had a very small amount of land to grow on. They went with high-yielding crops because they couldn't afford to grow anything else. Just like William was saying, so many people today don't have the savings to weather if a disaster strikes. But doing what you need to do in the moment without having a vision for the future—"

"Like us," said her husband, "trying to figure out what we're going to do now that I'm retiring."

"Okay then," agreed Betty, "like us, although we'll figure something out. I mean, that's why we're all here, to try to learn strategies now that will set us up for success—or at least buffer us from disaster—in the future."

Everyone was quiet for a moment. Then Rose spoke. "Peter and I went to Ireland on our honeymoon. Such a beautiful country! My grandmother was Irish and I had always wanted to visit—she told such stories about her home. It makes me sad to think that such a beautiful country suffered so much."

Peter took her hand. "Don't forget the resilience of the Irish," he said gently. "It was a terrible time, one we never want to see again, but it's still a wonderful country." He turned to the others. "Rose and I went to visit Munster in Ireland, the area her grandmother had grown up in. We went to Blarney Castle and kissed the famous Blarney Stone for luck. And let me tell you, it wasn't easy—you have to lie down over a cliff, grab some hand railings, and lean back. If you're lucky, someone hangs onto your belt to steady you."

Rose laughed. "You make it sound as if you risked life and limb." She turned to the others. "They have metal bars running across the opening. They keep you from falling."

"Another metaphor!" noted Sam. "Build in some handrails and metal bars—savings and multiple sources of income—to keep yourself from falling financially."

"I want to hear the rest of the story," said Gabriela. "When you kissed the stone, did you make a wish?"

"Yes!" said Rose. "And it came true. The next year, we gave birth to our wonderful son."

"And he became a doctor," Peter added with a smile.

"Peter, you know very well that wasn't part of my wish!" said Rose indignantly.

"Of course not!" He grinned. "It was mine. I love dropping the words 'my son, the doctor' into every conversation."

"The Blarney Stone also gave you the gift of a silver tongue," his wife remarked. "You can talk your way out of anything."

"Since we're talking of gifts," Peter continued, "let's not forget the greatest gift Ireland has ever given the world: you."

Rose blinked away tears as Peter kissed her hand. "That's my husband," she said to the group, smiling through the tears. "He's always looking for the silver lining."

"Maybe that's also an important strategy," Joe remarked. "Being optimistic. If you don't believe you can find a solution, you won't. For me, that's what is at the heart of everything we've learned so far: that there are so many opportunities available to us no matter where we are on the path to retirement, there's no reason to despair."

CHAPTER FIVE

ALL AT SEA

The Morning Ritual

That morning, Gabriela got up early so she could jog before meeting the other women in the piano lounge for coffee.

"Morning yoga is all well and good," she told them as she stirred milk into her coffee. "But jogging onboard a moving ship in the cool morning air? That's not something I'll be able to do once this trip is over."

"That's right," said Rose. "Make the most of it."

"That's a good philosophy for life," said Betty. "Make the most of it, no matter where you are."

"I try!" Maya laughed. "But wow—some mornings, trying to get the kids up and fed and dressed? I know in my heart that every moment is precious, but sometimes I'm too tired to notice!"

Shirley looked around at the women. "Not to be too personal," she said, "but it looks to me as if each of us is at a different point in life. I'm in my fifties, and Betty, if you don't mind me guessing, you may be a little ahead of me."

Betty grinned. "I don't mind at all. My mother always lied about her age, but I'm proud to look this good at sixty!"

Rose laughed. "My mother always said that a woman who didn't lie about her age had no imagination. But I find it easier to remember the truth, which is that I am seventy-three."

Gabriela smiled. "In the face of all this honesty, I won't try to shave any years off. I'm forty-two."

"And I'm thirty-four," Maya added. "Although having two little ones back-to-back has aged me."

"You get it back once they're in school," Shirley said. "And then they become teenagers and suddenly you're eighty—at least in their eyes!"

"Lamont and I don't have kids," Gabriela said. "Although we do have nieces and nephews. I highly recommend being the cool aunt!"

"They say having children changes your priorities," Maya said thoughtfully, "but I don't know if that's true. I know people who were selfish before they had kids and who are still selfish now that they have kids. And some of my friends who are great parents were already cool aunts and uncles before they had kids."

"I don't know that there's anything that changes people fundamentally, unless they want to change," Shirley said. "That's one of the things that worries me about retiring. It's going to force change on Sam and me, and I'm not sure either one of us is ready for that."

"May I join you?"

The women looked up to see Rachael, a cup of coffee in hand. Maya moved over to make room for another chair, and Rachael pulled a seat up to their table.

"I couldn't help but overhear," she said. "I think it's great that you're all thinking about how changes might affect you—and how they might not." She took a sip of her coffee. "I think a lot of the time, people expect the wrong things to have the greatest impact on your life. I'm not saying having children isn't a big change—any sleep-deprived parent will assure you that it is! But making small, steady decisions can have just as big an impact on your life, if not more so."

"Are you talking about things like saving for retirement?" Betty asked.

"Well, sure," admitted Rachael. "That's the name of the game on this cruise. But it's more than just making sure you have the resources to enjoy your golden years. When you set a certain amount of money aside every month earmarked for your future, over time, you become someone who thinks about your future in a positive, productive way. That doesn't just impact your life—it also has an impact on the lives of the people you love.

"For instance," she continued. "Let's say that you and your partner start talking about retirement when you're in your forties."

"That's me and Lamont!" Gabriela chimed in.

Rachael smiled. "Perfect. So you start thinking about what you want to do in, say, fifteen years. Maybe you'll decide to travel. You start having shared dreams about where you'll go, what adventures you'll have. You put money aside not because you have to, not because we tell you it's a smart thing to do, but because you have a shared vision of the fun you'll have and it makes sense to contribute to that to make it happen."

"Like having a vacation fund, where you put extra money in the cookie jar until you have enough to get away for a few days," said Betty.

"Exactly," agreed Rachael. "And when you're putting that money aside, yes, it might mean doing without something you'd like in the here and now, but you're committed as a couple to a shared vision of your future. Framing it in terms of building, of enabling something delicious you can look forward to—that strengthens a marriage in the moment while also doing the boring, long-term work of investing in your retirement."

"What about balancing work and family?" Maya asked. "That eats up way too much of my brain power."

"It's hard," Betty agreed. "I just made it work situation by situation."

"There's no one right answer," Rachael said. "Every family will make decisions that make sense to them. Some parents work separate shifts so that someone is always home when the kids aren't at school. Others have one parent—let's be honest, it's usually the mom—take time off of work when the children are little. Others hire help from the beginning, while still others rely on their parents or those cool aunts I heard you talking about. You almost can't have too much support when you're trying to build a career and raise a family.

"The only wrong choice," Rachael continued, "is to put off saving for your own retirement because you're overwhelmed by the demands of the moment. This is why you want to automate as much of it as you can: monthly automatic investments that come out of your account or, even better, straight from your paycheck into a retirement savings vehicle that you can't touch—that's the safest bet. You never want to waste brain power thinking each month about whether you'll have enough money to set some aside. Set it aside first and you'll find a way to live on what's left. And then it will be there when you need it down the line. As they say, your kids can get loans for college, but nobody is giving you a loan for retirement."

LECTURE 4: INFLATION

The women met up with their husbands on the deck. The fresh air and the blue sky made everything seem possible.

Maya was thinking about how she and Andrei were going to balance childcare once she went back to work full-time. She gave his hand a squeeze. He loved his kids, but he'd been so busy getting his startup running that he had missed a lot of the fun she'd had with them in their first few years. Maya was glad he would get the chance to spend a lot more time with them soon, although she was a little sad that she would be the one missing impromptu picnics in the park during the week. Still, she was glad to have the opportunity to build a career doing work she loved and was good at. Maya sighed. Balancing work and family was still taking up a lot of her brain power, she told herself ruefully.

They headed to the auditorium. They were a minute or two late, and William had already taken the stage.

"Today," William told his audience, "I will be talking about *inflation*. This is something you already know a good deal about: things that used to cost less money cost more money now. Or you pay the same amount, but for smaller portions of everything from soup cans to cereal boxes. In 1920, a cup of coffee at a diner cost you about fifteen cents; now it costs about two dollars. That's inflation in a nutshell: things cost more.

"Inflation reduces the real value of your monetary unit—in this case, the dollar. Looking at an overview of costs, in 2020, it took

$15.59 to buy the same amount of stuff that you could have gotten for a single dollar in 1930.

"Some types of items go up faster than others. The following chart shows the annual inflation rate from 1930 to 2020."

William clicked a remote and a slide appeared on the screen behind him.

ITEM	ANNUAL INFLATION RATE
Food/beverage	3.90%
Housing	4.19%
Apparel	1.79%
Transportation	3.17%
Medical care	5.12%
Recreation	1.10%

"According to the Bureau of Labor Statistics Consumer Price Index," he said, "prices in 2020 were 1,458.56 percent higher than the average price in 1930. How does that happen? It's not that it goes unnoticed, but it's also not something that most people worry about. Have you heard the story about how to cook a frog? If you put it in boiling water, it'll jump right out, but if you put it in tepid water and slowly heat it up, the frog doesn't notice that it's getting parboiled.

"I'm not sure if it's true or not, never having had any desire to boil a frog, but metaphorically, it is definitely true of human beings and inflation. We don't notice price changes as they happen because they creep up on us. It's only when things happen suddenly—gas prices, for instance, can jump very quickly—or when you see prices rising against the backdrop of a fixed budget that you notice it's getting harder and harder to pay for everything on your grocery list."

The audience murmured in alarm as they watched the dollar devalue right before their eyes. Everyone was thinking about what it would mean when they, too, were on a fixed budget. Struggling to get groceries was not how anyone hoped to spend their later years.

"Obviously," William said gently, "this is not the experience I want for any of you. And so we need to make sure that we take inflation into account when we plan for our future.

"There are ways to protect yourself," he continued. "The key way is to invest in things that will also go up over time. Inflation in housing prices, for instance, means your house is worth more as time goes on. Owning real estate therefore becomes one of the key ways to bolster your financial position. You can own your own home—I consider that to be a very good start—but you can also own rental property, which has the benefit not only of the property itself increasing in value, but the income from the property, the rental income, also increases with inflation. This is the opposite of fixed income: More money comes in as inflation rises and you, too, can charge more for goods and services.

"If you don't want to invest in real estate by owning property directly," William went on, "you can invest in things called real estate investment trusts, or REITs. Think of them like mutual funds, except instead of individuals pooling their money to buy stocks, you're using pooled resources to buy income-generating property. It's a way to invest in the housing boom without having to become a landlord. REITs aren't perfect—the value of your share doesn't appreciate in the same way your home would appreciate over time—but they can provide steady income. And they're far more liquid than an actual investment property, which you may not always be able to find a buyer for.

"You can also buy stocks in commodities that are likely to increase in value with inflation, things like oil or metals. Now, nothing Gunnar or Rachael or I say should be interpreted as financial advice. We're not saying go out and bet the farm on commodities. Everyone's financial situation is different. But we do suggest you look at investing in things that appreciate over time as part of a balanced portfolio. Individual stocks, bonds, commodities, mutual funds, REITs, annuities—they all may have a place in your financial future.

"In that same vein," William continued, "mutual funds can help you create a diverse portfolio. Here, the shares may also increase in value or they may not, but they might instead provide dividends to increase your income. The idea of pooling your money with other investors to buy shares of companies allows you to have a piece of what once was a pie only the wealthy could afford a slice of.

"When you are saving for retirement, there is a lot to be said for looking at index funds, which simply mimic something like the Dow Jones Industrial Average. They don't try to beat the market; they're content with mimicking the market—and that's not a bad return on investment. Evaluate every mutual fund by looking at past performance and its investment philosophy. It's important to find ones that fit your needs and your capacity for risk. I would be careful of putting much money in a brand-new mutual fund. It's not that they're inherently bad, only that you have less data to evaluate on something new. With money you're willing to gamble, you can take a flier on anything, be it a new mutual fund or an individual stock or even an initial public offering, or IPO. But with funds you're going to need in your retirement, slow and steady really does win the race."

He looked around the room. "So how do you invest in something like REITs or mutual funds? I recommend something called *dollar cost averaging*, where you automatically invest a certain amount every month. When the share prices go down, your money buys more shares. When prices go up, your monthly investment buys fewer shares, but they are each worth more. The last thing you want to do is try to time the market. That's closer to gambling than it is to investing, and as we learned earlier in the cruise, you never want to gamble with your financial future."

William took a moment to look out at the crowd. "For those of you on the younger side," he said, "dollar cost averaging is the way to go. You want to put some money aside every month, ideally directly from your paycheck, but if not, then as quickly as possible out of your bank account. It should be a fixed amount that goes immediately into an IRA or a brokerage account that's hard for you to access. The more you can keep that money out of sight, the more likely it is to be there, intact, when you need it in twenty or thirty years. Think of it as paying yourself first. Ben Franklin said, 'A penny saved is a penny earned.' I'd go farther and say that a penny saved *and invested* is the first step to safety, comfort, and freedom in your golden years."

Gabriela thought back to Rachael's advice that morning—what Betty had called "putting money in the cookie jar." She thought about how having an exciting vision for their future would make it easier for her and Lamont to set that money aside, and decided to speak to him about Rachael's ideas as soon as the lecture was over. Betty, too, thought about her cookie jar analogy. The only difference, she thought ruefully, was that the cookie jar did not give her interest on her investment.

"There is one specific kind of inflation I want to mention, and then I will let you go enjoy your afternoon at sea," William said. "That is *stagflation*. Think of stagflation as inflation on steroids: prices for goods and services rise quickly and to higher levels than what we've come to think of as normal inflation. Worse, it is coupled with a stagnant economy—that's obviously the "stag" part of stagflation, and not a stag party or a stag beetle, I regret to say. We economists are not generally given to flights of fancy!"

The audience smiled and William went on. "So the problem is this: You have unemployment, sometimes quite high unemployment, which means a stagnant economy and a decline in your gross domestic product, or the value of the goods your country provides. Normally, we would expect unemployment and depressed wages to lead to a decreased demand for goods; people have less money to spend, so there is less of a demand for goods and services. The economy slows down and we might even expect to see *deflation*, which is the opposite of inflation: A dollar would buy more today than it did yesterday.

"Stagflation upends that expectation. It's when we have a gloomy economy coupled with rising prices. It came to the forefront in the mid-1970s, when the oil crisis helped trigger a recession that led to double-digit inflation coupled with nearly double-digit unemployment, and that was bad news for the economy. It's also tricky to solve, and it's really out of an individual's hands. That's something I want you all to consider: The brightest economic minds sometimes muck around, doing their best, but still come up against an intractable cycle that can have an impact on your individual life. This is why our team will, time and again, suggest having a liquid emergency fund and a diverse portfolio. Because there will always be surreal economic times that you'll just have to ride out.

"But for today," William wrapped up, "I want you to digest all this information and enjoy your own ride on this wonderful ship. Key take-aways are: first, to remain diversified; second, to include investments that will themselves rise in value with inflation; third, to have an emergency fund that can tide you over in an economic downturn; and finally, to pay yourself first and, ideally, automatically so you never have to think about it again. The earlier you start, the more secure you'll be, but even if you are on retirement's doorstep, these are strategies that will help keep you on an even keel throughout your retirement. I look forward to seeing you all tomorrow."

Dinner: The Captain's Table

The couples met up for drinks before dinner. Although the day of cruising on the water had been lovely, they were all a little subdued.

"There was so much to grapple with from today's lecture," said Peter, giving voice to what they were all thinking.

"It feels like an awful lot is out of our control," said Shirley.

Her husband nodded. "That was my feeling when William was talking about cycles," he agreed. "There are such major forces in play, global forces, and it seems impossible to deal with them."

"Maybe the key is not trying to change them," Lamont said, "but navigate them. Like surfing a wave. You don't control the wave, but you control your experience on the wave by adjusting to it as you ride."

"Or for those of us a little too old to surf," laughed Rose, "we might look at it like steering a ship."

"I like that idea," agreed Sam. "We can't control these larger forces, but we can control how we ride them out. And maybe, like timing the market, we don't have to worry too much about predicting what will happen—we just need to keep our options open so that whatever does happen, we have something in our financial tool kit to get us through."

At that moment, a crewmember came to ask them if they would care to join the captain for dinner. The group was delighted and moved into the dining room to take their places at the captain's table.

Captain Genevieve Olson and Chief Mate Eddie DeSalle were delightful dinner companions. Both spoke of their lifelong dream of working on a ship. Chief Mate DeSalle was a local, having grown up along the banks of the Mississippi, and was looking forward to captaining his own riverboat someday. Captain Olson was Norwegian. She had studied extensively both abroad and in the United States, and while she loved being a riverboat captain, her hobby was hydrography.

"When people think of those who study the oceans," she explained, "they usually think of oceanographers, people who study the creatures and plants that live in the water. But hydrographers study the water itself and the mapping of the ocean floor." She beamed at them. "It is a fascinating study. For a long time, each country had their own symbols for ocean maps. It was difficult for sailors from one country to read maps created by another country. It was only about a hundred years ago that the nations of the world got together to standardize maps, so that a French sailor could read a Dutch map while sailing through international waters."

"That feels a little like what we're doing here," said Andrei. "Each of us has our own guideposts and our own shoals, if you will. The tricky part is learning from each other's maps how to get through our own rapids." He grinned. "Forgive the mixed metaphors!"

"Not at all," said DeSalle. "At least you kept it all nautical."

"You know," said Betty, "as an English teacher, I have learned that there are a lot of common terms that have nautical origins. In fact, I was just thinking about William's lecture today. He mentioned that an emergency fund could 'tide us over' during an economic downturn. That's actually nautical! When the wind wasn't blowing, the ship floated forward on the tide alone, and so it came to mean making do with just a little bit until things got better."

"And when you're faced with a sudden economic downturn," said Rose, "it makes sense to batten down the hatches."

"We're on this cruise to learn the ropes," added Sam, getting into the game.

"Even though some of it is hard to fathom!" Maya joined in.

"But the goal," Peter agreed, "is to get our finances in shipshape."

"I'll admit," laughed Lamont as the game wound down, "that William's discussion of stagflation had me all at sea!"

Chapter Six

BEST PRACTICES

The Morning Ritual

Sam, Peter, Lamont, Joe, and Andrei met up again to walk around the deck. They had known each other for less than a week, but already they felt comfortable together.

"The problem with taking a cruise about getting ready for retirement," said Andrei, "is that cruises are supposed to be about relaxation, and when I think about money, all I feel is stress."

"Retirement doesn't stress me out," said Joe. "Work does. My boss is always pressuring me for more production, and then our reward for making their quotas is to see half the staff get laid off the minute there's a downtick. The stress was there all the time: Would we produce enough? Would we make it through without cuts? Would I get laid off? And what really made me mad was that none of that stress was good for the work itself. I wasn't stressing over finding ways to make stuff better. I was stressing over what people in the front office might do or not do. Oh, no," he said, "there's nothing about retirement that stresses me as much as the day-in, day-out worry about things I have no control over. Me, I can't wait to be retired."

Andrei smiled grimly. "Try being the one who has control over everything," he said. "Starting a business is crazy. There are thousands of decisions to be made every day and you really don't know which are the right ones. You just make the best decision you can and then be willing to change course if you find out you're wrong."

"That sounds like a good plan for life," Lamont said. "I mean, none of us really knows what's going to happen—what's going to work out financially or pop artistically. We're all just doing the best we can and hopefully we're in a position to pivot when things go haywire."

"The same is true in my line," agreed Sam. "It's really tough to tell how gift shop items will sell. I'm not just talking what specific item will sell—because you're right, Lamont, there's no way to tell what's going to be the next craze and what's just going to fizzle out—but whether anything will sell at all. For instance, you would think if the economy is doing well, gifts would go up. If the economy is going downhill, gifts would go down. Right?"

"I would think that," agreed Peter.

"And you'd be wrong." Sam laughed. "People are a lot more complicated than that. Sometimes it works that way, but sometimes when people have more money to spend, they spend it on more expensive things. They don't shop as much in the kinds of stores we service, or if they do, it's just for birthday or holiday cards. They get their gifts from someplace a little more upmarket. On the other hand, in down times, when people have to put big plans on hold, they're more likely to make an impulse buy and get a gift for themselves or for someone they love. They tell themselves, 'I can't afford a vacation this year, but I can get myself this cute teddy bear' or 'I have this birthday present I need to buy, and this gift looks beautiful but it's not crazy expensive.' And so they'll pick up something along with the card."

"That must be frustrating when your job is on commission," Lamont said.

"It is." Sam sighed. "When gifts don't turn over, I don't make as much, plus some shop owners don't understand that these things are cyclical. They think there's something wrong with the gifts, or maybe that there's not enough variety. Whatever it is, they think it's my fault. Everybody gets very grumpy when their livelihood is on the line."

"Maybe that's the best reason to make sure you're secure in

retirement," Peter said thoughtfully. "If you're worried about money, it's pretty hard to be living as your best self."

LECTURE 5: RECESSION

William's next lecture was scheduled for late afternoon, and no one lingered on shore; everyone wanted to make sure they were in their seats when he started. The topic of the day was recession.

"First, let's give a definition or two. *Recession* is a term used for an economic decline that lasts several months. Recessions can be local to one country or they can be global. There are a lot of theories about what causes recessions, and they run the gamut from purely economic reasons all the way to social and psychological reasons. In practice, they can be triggered by several ongoing trends or by one big, sudden economic shock, such as the 2020 pandemic. We had a recession when we transitioned to a peacetime economy after World War II, and we've had them when monetary policy has been tightened because of a fear of inflation. Recessions have been sparked by oil crises, consumer pessimism, dot-com bubbles, stock market crashes, and the subprime mortgage crisis. And while theories abound as to what to do to speed recovery—things like printing more dollars, encouraging consumer spending, and creating jobs with government investment in infrastructure such as dams, roads, and bridges—the economy is, in fact, a very fragile thing with many, many moving parts.

"It is impossible to control every aspect, to keep all those external and internal forces in balance, and so recessions need to be seen as inevitable. Gross domestic product goes down and unemployment goes up. There's a slowdown in buying, a decline in housing and major purchases, sometimes even a stock market crash. Recessions are not fun times.

"However, there is good news: Recessions are temporary. In general and over the long term, economies tend toward growth. Recessions happen all the time. Mostly they are bumps in the road—which doesn't mean they're necessarily easy to weather. But it does mean you have to figure them into your plans. If you're going to be around a long time, and I hope you all are, your retirement is going to include one or two or more recessions. And possibly even a depression, which is a recession that is particularly deep—the Great Depression saw unemployment rates up to 27 percent—and lasts years instead of months."

William stopped to take the pulse of his audience. No one looked happy at what he had phrased as "good news."

"Look, I would be doing you a disservice if I pretended the economy was only ever going to go up. And you would be setting yourself up for disaster to pretend the same. There's no need to wear blinders. What you really need to do is to understand the cyclical nature of the economy and put together a plan for how you're going to make it through the down times.

"Here are some ways you can build your own financial safety net, one that will see you through an economic downturn.

"First, hold onto your real estate. If you can, acquire more. Real estate values reliably go up over time. I know Gunnar has talked to you about having an emergency fund, and if you're going to be buying property—especially if you're going to be leveraging your equity to buy more property—you want to have your emergency savings set up before you do. It's tempting to buy the biggest house the lender will let you buy, but that's not necessarily the size house you can afford. The subprime mortgage crisis was a real eye-opener in terms of how many people were able to borrow more money than they could really afford, and the recession that followed that particular collapse saw a lot of people lose their home. Let's not do that.

"As for me," William continued, "I am a big believer in real estate. When I bought my first apartment complex, however, my emergency safety net was my own home. I knew I could sell it if I had to and move my family into one of my own units. Would that have been my first choice? Definitely not. But it was a solid Plan B. You need to have a Plan B that does not involve you and your family living in a shelter somewhere. Also, I should say I have a pretty big risk tolerance. Yours will vary. And that's okay. Again, you have to enjoy the journey.

"But it's worth at least looking into real estate because land is finite and valuable, which means it is almost guaranteed to appreciate over the long haul. If you don't want to risk quite as much as I did when I started acquiring apartment complexes, you can look into REITs, or real estate investment trusts, which I mentioned briefly in yesterday's lecture. REITs are a little like mutual funds for real estate. They are excellent for smaller investors, allowing you to get in on the real estate market without having to come up with a down payment. They also provide diversification. Even if you decide that becoming a landlord is your life's calling, you can only own a few properties. REITs allow you to invest in a much wider variety."

William paused to take a drink of water. Shirley noticed that her husband was taking copious notes. She thought about their duplex and how they really hadn't invested any time or energy into making it homey, much less turning it into a real investment opportunity. She smiled as she caught Sam's eye. She could tell her husband was seriously considering diving into real estate investments.

"Okay, so real estate is the first way to recession-proof your wealth," William continued. "At the very least, hang onto your home as long as you can. You have to live somewhere, and in addition to it appreciating in value, when you own your home, you can rent out a room to a college student for the school year, or in short-term bursts to visiting tourists on one of the many home-as-hotel sites. I know a lot of people in Augusta, Georgia, who take their vacation every spring to coincide with the Masters Tournament, so while they're frolicking on the beach, they're renting out their home to the golf-loving crowds who descend on Augusta for that one week. Owning your home provides many flexible ways to create income as well as protect wealth.

"Second, use excess capital to buy stock in commodities. This, of course, is not specific investing advice—always do your own due diligence—but commodities ranging from oil to utilities have historically gone up. Take a look at what you can't live without, and chances are other people will continue to need those things as well.

"Third, buy bonds. Bonds are not sexy. If you hold them to maturity, what do you generally get back? You get back your initial investment. Ho-hum. So why buy bonds? Because bonds will give you an interest income, often twice a year, until they reach maturity. You preserve your entire capital by holding the bonds until they mature, and in the meantime, you get reliable, predictable interest income. Government bonds generally have very low risk, but bonds are not risk-free. Most bonds issued by local or even national governments are unlikely to default, but the interest rates are often low.

"If the rate of inflation is high, you also risk having less spending power when you recoup your principal at maturity. If interest rates go up, you might want to reclaim that money to invest elsewhere, but to do that, you'll have to find a buyer, and you might even have to sell at a discount.

"Finally, corporate bonds may have higher interest rates, but bonds are essentially loans—and just like your brother-in-law might not pay you back that twenty he owes, some companies may end up defaulting on their bonds.

"Stocks, bonds, and real estate—all, I believe, have a place in your portfolio. They balance each other out and give you the most flexibility whether the economy is booming or busting. I'll talk more on another day about investing options, because I know that's a big reason you've all taken this cruise, but I also want to hammer home the idea that investing, while important, is not your only recourse. For those of you who don't have excess income to invest yet, you still need to take care to protect yourself in the case of a downturn. Nothing makes me sadder than to see people struggling to make their mortgage after a job loss or an illness or a recession. You can't assume that everything will go well all the time. In fact, I believe you should prepare for the worst."

William paused for another sip of water. Joe leaned over to his wife, who was taking notes on her laptop. "He's in a real positive mood today, isn't he?" he whispered.

"It's just what I tell my students," Betty whispered back. "Get the phone numbers of friends who can help you when you forget the homework assignment on the first day of school, not by posting online at midnight the night before it's due. Figure out what tutoring is available at your school before you start failing the quizzes. Do the extra credit even if you have an A, so that one bombed test doesn't wreck your GPA."

"We might've needed to do that a little more," Joe admitted.

"Maybe, but at least we didn't wait until after we'd run through our savings," Betty replied.

Joe looked like he was going to say more, but his wife shushed him. William had started speaking again.

"So how do you do that?" William asked. "How do you prepare for the worst when you're already most likely spending your paycheck as it comes in?

"No one is going to like this part, I'll warn you about that upfront, but this is the cornerstone of creating wealth: Change your lifestyle until you have more money coming in than you have going out. Use that difference to pay off debt, build an emergency fund, and start an investment fund with which you will build your future.

"Note that I'm not telling you how to change your lifestyle. That part is up to you. And maybe Gunnar—always check with him, he has a lot of great ideas—I know he talked to you today about ways to cut expenses and increase income, and I'm going to try not to duplicate him too much." He paused and gave a little laugh. "Generally, my recommendations are a little more next-level—saving on steroids—so brace yourselves.

"There is a two-pronged approach to having more income than outgo, and I recommend you always do both.

"First, cut your expenses. Track them for a month to see where your money is going and then be ruthless. Look at any recurring charges to see if, in fact, you really need that online magazine or membership. Don't get rid of things you love, but get real about things you *think* you should love or should do. Gym memberships spring to mind. Don't keep paying every month because you imagine that someday you'll become a person who goes to the gym every day. Either become that person now or cancel the membership; you can always rejoin if fitness does become your priority. Right now, however, especially if you don't have a lot of capital to invest, let's decide that your financial safety net is your priority. You can always run in the park; you don't want to end up sleeping there.

"Start by cutting out all those recurring expenses that seemed like a good idea at the time, but that you're not really taking advantage of. Then start to trim down your discretionary spending. Eating out two or three times a week? Cut it down to twice a month. Pack your own lunches; you will be astounded how much money that saves. Stop buying new things—just stop it entirely. Make the decision to make do with what you have for the next year in terms of clothes, phones, gadgets, furniture. Do you really need both of your cars? Sell one. Take public transportation or carpool as much as possible. Move to another part of the country where housing, utilities, and property taxes are lower.

"Second, how can you increase your income? Gunnar is great at this; make use of him. I'll just add that you are probably not maximizing your professional expertise. This is crucial. Doubling down on what you already do well and looking to that arena first can only increase your reputation and your professional value to others. You need to advocate for that promotion or raise. Additional duties might be taken on for extra income, either on the side or as overtime. Constantly scan for ways to leverage your expertise for your current employer, for a more lucrative position, or for other jobs after hours.

"All additional income and savings go straight into one of three buckets: paying off debt; building an emergency fund that can cover six months of expenses; or building an investment fund. We'll talk about where that money might best serve you in a later lecture.

"Does this all sound draconian? It might be. But if you are living on the edge of your income, you are one setback away from disaster. If a recession turns into a depression, having taken steps like these when times were prosperous could be the difference between keeping your house and finding yourself in foreclosure. So many people found themselves underwater when property values took a nosedive in 2008. Those who couldn't continue to make their mortgage or pay their property taxes had a hard time recouping the money they'd put into the house, let alone preserving capital or keeping their real estate.

"Look, if you already have enough money to do everything you want to over a thirty- or forty-year retirement, then enjoy your cruise and remember to tip the stewards well. You don't need to be in this room. But most of you aren't there yet. You don't have to do everything I've suggested—although if you're game, don't let me talk you out of it—but I recommend that all of you think hard about what choices you can make now that will pay big dividends down the line. Take on one way of cutting your budget and one way of making more money, and be relentless about those for three months. Once they become a habit—and once you can see that doing without that new phone translates directly into having money to invest in an opportunity that excites you—you may find yourself motivated to add new ways to save even more.

"And, yes, I am making a big ask here: I'm asking you to re-evaluate your priorities in life. Instead of trying to keep up with the guy next door, or with the airbrushed, curated pictures you see on social media, I want you to evaluate everything through the lens of 'Am I setting myself up for financial success?' I don't want you to have the trappings of wealth. I want you to have the security of knowing you can make it through a rough patch. That is the true value of wealth—to allow you peace of mind and security.

"I will end today with this thought: You can choose to think of prioritizing your financial success as difficult, as punishing, as deprivation. The price of those thoughts is financial security, because you are human and you will always, always rebel against rules you perceive as harsh or unfair. But there is another way to think of all of this, and that is as an opportunity to enjoy what you already have. You have so much—you have people you love, creative skills you enjoy, a wide world to walk and appreciate. Delight in all of it while giving yourself the tremendous gift of financial flexibility that will allow you to roll with the punches and weather the storms."

Shore Leave: Vicksburg

Rather than going into the town of Vicksburg itself, Gabriela and Lamont decided to do one of the ship's excursions: kayaking along the Mississippi Delta. A guide met them and several other couples for a quick safety presentation before showing them to the kayaks.

"I don't know about this," said Lamont as they got into their two-person kayak.

"Relax," answered his wife. "The write-up said 'no experience necessary.' You just have to be willing to paddle."

"And wear a life vest," Lamont pointed out. "Making me wear this life vest implicitly means we could drown."

"No," Gabriela corrected, "it explicitly means that you may get dunked, but it's very unlikely that you will drown. And why is that? Because you will be wearing a life vest."

They paddled off with their group. The plan was to paddle a few miles upriver with their guide, meet up with a picnic dinner that would be set up for them on the shore, then paddle back downstream at sunset. It would be particularly special on the water tonight, the guide had told them, because there would be a full moon.

It took Lamont and Gabriela a little while to get into the rhythm of paddling together. There was a lot of splashing and laughter, and a good amount of elbow grease needed to keep them in the middle of the pack.

"We're going to feel this tomorrow!" Gabriela laughed as they pulled on their paddles.

"True, we're using muscles we don't normally think about," Lamont agreed. "Although it's actually not as much work as I thought it would be."

"It's the way the water eddies," Gabriela said. "I heard the guide talking about it. That little bit of—would you call it a current? Anyway, it helps us along."

Lamont was quiet for a moment. "This is another metaphor, isn't it?"

"What do you mean?"

"Paddling," he explained. "It's another metaphor for our financial future. Look at how we started out. I was very nervous and maybe a little overly cautious—"

"Maybe a little!" his wife teased.

"And you," he pointed out, "were maybe a little overly confident. This is harder than you thought it would be, but not as bad as I imagined. Both overconfidence and too much of a fear of risk would keep us from succeeding on this trip. Luckily, we balanced each other out and were both willing to take the risk, while also being prepared for how hard it might be. We supported each other in this."

"We do make a good team," Gabriela agreed.

"And then," Lamont said, warming to his idea, "we got into a rhythm of paddling together and we're moving forward. Just like once we make decisions about our financial future and put some things in place, like fully funding our IRAs, for instance . . . ."

Gabriela looked surprised. "I didn't know you were thinking about that."

Lamont shrugged. "It seems like a no-brainer of a first step. I know we've been putting everything into growing your business, but I think we need to start investing in a safety net as well."

"So once we do that, you're saying it'll be like now, paddling upriver?"

"Yes, with the eddy—of stock appreciation, compound interest, dividends—to help us."

Gabriela was so surprised she stopped paddling for a minute. "Do you even know what those things are?"

Lamont smiled. "Just because I'm an artist doesn't mean I can't comprehend numbers. I'm pretty good at math, in fact, and I spent yesterday afternoon in the ship's library checking out some books on the basics of investing."

Gabriela put her paddle back in the water and gave an extra-hard push. "You are full of surprises," she said. "I'm happy we're on the same team."

"Me, too," Lamont said. "Hey, is that the picnic spot up ahead? This really was easier to reach than I thought it would be."

"Let's hope our financial goals are the same," she answered as they headed for the shore.

Later that evening, after a relaxing picnic, they got back in their kayaks. The air was cooling as they started paddling downstream, back to their ship.

"This is glorious," said Gabriela, taking in the starry sky and rising moon.

"You're right," agreed Lamont. "I take back everything I said before we started out today. Taking a risk on this trip was the best decision we could have made."

WE ARE ALL DIFFERENT AND THE SAME

Betty and Joe had done a quick tour of Vicksburg and had returned to the boat early. When they got back, they discovered that Gunnar was giving a mini lecture in the library to those who had chosen not to go on one of the shore tours. Eager to learn more after their Reality Check, they helped themselves to iced tea from a service by the door and settled into some of the comfortable chairs that had been set up for the audience. The small space and the chairs arranged in concentric semicircles made it an intimate setting for the lecture, and Joe and Betty felt almost as if Gunnar were talking only to them.

Gunnar smiled as the dozen or so passengers took their seats. "I'm delighted to see you here today," he said, "and I'm going to try to make this worth missing a shore excursion. So here's the important point up front: There is no one-size-fits-all answer for retirement, but there *are* 'best practices.'" He grinned at them. "That's the key takeaway, so if you want to run off and get a quick view of Vicksburg, you can leave now."

The audience smiled. Gunnar looked around. No one got up to leave.

"Excellent," he said, "because there's a little more.

"We are all the same, but we are also all different. That's maybe the easiest thing to see, our differences. Every person I work with has a different financial portfolio, a different tolerance for risk, a different set of expectations for retirement, and any number of different priorities for how to spend their time and their money. And there are many different solutions for every problem you face. But there are a certain number of best practices that you can put into place no matter where you are financially or what you want to do with your golden years.

"First, you can save more. You *should* save more. We are human beings with human brains; if you have a certain amount coming in, you can bet that you'll make plans for that money to go out. Even people who budget don't generally budget in regular and sufficient savings. This is the first place to start, no matter what else is going on in your life, because saving doesn't happen to you—you have to make it happen.

"One way to trick yourself into saving is to think of it not as saving, but as 'paying yourself first.' You want to put aside some part of every paycheck—and I'm including those of you who are self-employed—into an account that's earmarked for retirement. It should be money that's hard to access until you're ready for retirement, because if it's easy to take the money out, you probably will take it out. There will always be a desire big enough or an emergency critical enough to make you deplete that account if you can. But here's the thing: Retirement itself is going to be that kind of emergency. Having financial stability is going to be that big a desire. And if that money is used up ahead of retirement, you are going to have very few options when you're in your sixties or seventies to live the rest of your life on your own terms."

He paused to take a look around the room. Betty realized that Maya was also there in the front row; she saw the younger woman raise her hand.

"But Gunnar," Maya asked, "what if there *is* an emergency? If that money isn't accessible, how would we manage? Don't we want to be able to reach our money if we really need it?"

"That is a great question, Maya," he replied. "And one I was hoping would be asked. Because, in fact, a lot of us live our lives that way, going from one financial emergency to another. We mentioned this earlier on the cruise, but it bears repeating because it's the cornerstone of the problem: Most Americans don't have enough in savings to cover a $1,000 emergency expense. Not having enough savings leaves you open to being exploited by financial companies, from credit card interest rates of 16 percent or more to payday loans, which have interest rates ranging from 36 percent to a whopping 600 percent, or even more."

Joe gasped. He had seen ads for payday loans, but had no idea they could charge that much in interest.

Gunnar continued. "The best way to protect yourself," he said, "is to make building your savings a priority. Your retirement savings is not the same as your emergency savings. And, yes, you should build your emergency savings first and aggressively, but that doesn't mean you can't already start saving a little bit in retirement right away. Again, you don't want all your savings to be within easy reach or you will probably reach once too often.

"So how do you go about building your savings?" he asked. "Step one is to figure out how much you have in fixed expenses: rent, utilities, things like that. Groceries can be tricky; you can probably spend less on groceries than you currently do, but if you offset that by eating out because you're bored with a week of bean soup, you're not really saving anything. I suggest looking at how much you've spent on groceries over the last few months and averaging it out.

"Step two is to figure out if you're making enough to sustain the lifestyle you are living. You would be surprised how many people don't actually bring in enough to cover their expenses. This is a bad idea in the short term, and completely unsustainable over any length of time. If you are unemployed or underemployed, now is the time to take stock. What can you do to make yourself more attractive to employers offering better jobs, or to your current employer if a promotion is on the line? Can you pick up a second job temporarily or start a side gig doing something you're good at? Within your professional field, there are probably things you are extremely good at that someone will pay you to do; outside of your professional field, you probably have interests and abilities that range from walking dogs to making jewelry to teaching webinars. You don't need to make a lot of money, but if you can find a way to make just a little more, allocating all of it to savings will make your nest egg grow.

"Later in the cruise we're going to circle back to making more money, but for right now, I don't want to lose sight of saving, which is key. Once you know you have your necessities taken care of, you need to make building your emergency savings a priority. Start by deciding that for three months, you are going to save every extra dollar you can. Instead of going out with friends, organize a potluck or a picnic. We have access on our phones to more entertainment than our grandparents encountered in a lifetime; you can skip movies, concerts, theater, and other shows for three months. Lock your credit card away. Make it as difficult as possible for yourself to spend money for a finite period of time. Challenge yourself to weekly goals; do it with a friend and compete to see who can save the most. Make saving money a game.

"What you're aiming for is an emergency savings fund that can cover three months of living expenses—and you know what that amounts to because you just figured it out in step one. Let me reiterate: No matter where you are in life, from your first job to staring retirement in the face, if you do not have an emergency savings account, you need to take this step now. It's important to build your safety net *before* you need it; if you wait until it's time to jump, the results will not be pretty.

"One quick aside: A lot of people advocate an emergency fund that will cover six months of expenses. If you can pull that off, that's great, but I say start with three months. That will give you time to find temporary work, get a roommate, or do any of a hundred other things that can improve your financial situation. A six-month cushion gives you more time, but if you make the goalposts too far away, you might give it up as impossible and save nothing, and that, my friends, would be a fatal mistake. So start with saving up three months' worth of living expenses and add onto it a little at a time."

Gunnar took a second to look around the room. Some people were nodding while others were shaking their heads.

"I know," he said. "It seems like I'm advocating austerity measures that are impossible to live by. But remember, I'm just asking you to do it for a short amount of time while you build your emergency fund. If you think of it as punishment, you'll never do it. And maybe you'll get lucky and not need it, but it's far better to be prepared than to trust luck.

"So the trick here is to think about it not as an emergency fund, but as an adventure fund. Having that financial cushion opens the world to you. Once you've started saving, you'll realize that having a little extra money in the bank means that you can take advantage of a business opportunity when it comes along. You can have the flexibility to start a side hustle or go back to school or invest in business. Saving doesn't make your life small; on the contrary, it opens up a world of possibilities.

"Saving to get your financial cushion in place also teaches you to save. You'll see what a difference saving makes to your emergency fund. You'll also see how little difference there is in your everyday enjoyment of life when you've socked that money away rather than spent it. If you're someone who finds fun, you will find it everywhere—even on the cheap. And you'll enjoy the things you do spend money on even more if it's a choice instead of a mindless default because, say, Takeout Tuesdays or retail therapy is what's sold to you as a solution to your exhaustion. Go take a nap! That's free and guaranteed to be without either indigestion or buyer's remorse."

Gunnar rubbed his hands together. "Okay, I've talked enough about savings. Make it a game to get that emergency fund in place and start paying yourself first by putting money into some kind of savings vehicle for retirement. Traditional IRAs, Roth IRAs, SEP IRAs, 401K plans, and their ilk—those are all possible options. Look into how much the government allows you to put into them annually—it depends on your age—then divide that annual amount by twelve and have the money transferred from your bank account to a retirement account automatically every month. The more it can happen without you having to do anything active, the better.

"Saving aggressively is the first Best Practice. The second Best Practice is to set a goal for yourself, a goal of what you want retirement to look like. Why is this important? Because it gives you a vision to live into. Whether you want to make a million dollars, own a hundred rental units, sail the Mediterranean, or have a home with a backyard to garden in, having a vision that lights you up means that when you do something hard, like taking great care of your ten-year-old car instead of leasing the latest model, you know in your heart it's for a bigger purpose."

"The third Best Practice—and the one I'll leave you with today—is to invest in yourself. Believe in yourself and double down on what you do well. You're going to make mistakes, that's inevitable, but if you always believe that you will find a way out of them, or at least a way to learn from them, you will come back stronger. Don't let anything or anyone convince you that you shouldn't have the front office, that you shouldn't try for a promotion, that you shouldn't start your own business. Put in the time to learn how to understand financial statements, prospectuses, business plans. Find people who are doing what you want to do and ask them for advice. People love to be seen as experts! Most folks, like William and Rachael and me, love to help others with advice and guidance. It's how we give back to the world."

Gunnar smiled as he looked around at the group. "Everyone in this room probably wants different things from retirement—to travel, to stay at home, to pursue their passions, to help raise their grandchildren—but the one thing everyone wants is the freedom to not have to worry that they will outlive their savings. Implement these three best practices and you'll be on your way to building the kind of future you will be excited to live into."

Dinner: Á la Française

While Gabriela and Lamont picnicked with their tour group, the other couples met in the dining room. The whole room had been decorated as if it were in the heart of Paris. Candles were lit at every table, the menus were decorated with Eiffel Towers, and the piano had been wheeled in from the piano bar. A chanteuse performed as Edith Piaf while drinks were poured and waiters took their orders.

"I'm enjoying learning about the economy and what we can do to protect ourselves in retirement," said Betty. "But what I'm really going to miss when this cruise is over is the food!"

Everybody laughed. Maya dug into her roast duck à l'orange, savoring every bite.

"I like to cook," she said. "In fact, at one point I thought I might want to become a chef instead of a lawyer."

"You could be both," teased her husband. "I wouldn't mind coming home to glazed short ribs or Basque-style chicken with wine sauce every night."

"Then we're going to need a small army to take care of the kids and the house," she countered. "Not to mention a few sous-chefs. Maybe you could make me an app for that?"

Andrei took it good-naturedly. "I'll bring that up at our next creative meeting."

"You laugh," Rose said, "but it is crazy how much work goes into raising a family."

"I don't laugh!" Andrei protested. "I am grateful Maya was willing to put her career on hold so we could have a family. And now that my business is on more solid ground, I'm looking forward to supporting her as she spends more time with her own clients. But I'm not the one who wanted to be a chef!"

Peter shook his head. "I foresee a lot of franks and beans in your future," he told Maya.

They were interrupted by Chef Luigi as he and his team came out of the kitchen and headed toward the stage.

"I told you, you need sous-chefs!" Maya whispered as half a dozen people in white uniforms lined up behind the head chef.

"*Mes amis*!" Chef Luigi began, "I hope you are enjoying dinner this evening."

There was immediate and enthusiastic applause.

"I wanted to let you know that although I am named Luigi after my Italian father, my mother was French, and it is to her that I owe many of tonight's recipes, as well as my love of cooking.

"Many of you are parents, and I want you to know, you have more influence over your children than you think you do. I know my father shared with me his creativity and his zest for life, while my mother taught me the value of mastering the basics before trying to ad-lib, shall we say, and create a masterpiece of one's own.

"Since this is the financial cruise, William has asked me if I could connect my little speech to monetary matters. So I offer you this: First, do not skimp on the details that make the meal. Spend your money where it will give you the most happiness, whether that be a succulent piece of meat for the centerpiece of your dish or a cruise where you can reconnect with your loved ones. Or perhaps a garden, where you find the most bliss. A kitchen garden, of course!"

There was a ripple of laughter.

"Chef Luigi knows his audience," Sam whispered.

Luigi held up his hand for silence. "Second," he said, "I want to go back to what I said about children learning from their parents. Your little ones, and not-so-little ones, will have picked up more from what you do than from what you say, from how you live than from how you tell them to live. Your relationship with money will inevitably become their relationship with money—including your mistakes and your fears. The good news is that as you develop more confidence around financial matters, that confidence, too, will translate to the next generation. It is never too late to change your own financial future or to influence that of your children.

"And now, *bon appétit*!"

He gave a slight bow and the room erupted into applause.

Joe shook his head. "They never miss an opportunity to make us think about money, do they?"

"It's not really money they want us to think about," Rose said. "It's our future. It just so happens that the two go hand in hand."

"That's true," Betty said. "When we talked to Gunnar today, he gave us some good ideas for ways to improve our finances moving forward, but more importantly, he made us think about the kind of life we want to live. Between work and the kids and, well, all the other things life throws at us, I don't know that Joe and I have ever had a discussion about how we envision retirement."

"For all I know," Joe added, "Betty wants to buy an RV and travel the country."

Betty snorted. "If we're going to travel, it had better be to Europe."

Joe looked surprised. "Really?"

"Absolutely."

Peter laughed. "It looks like William's strategy to get us talking about our futures is working," he said.

"Almost anything is a better plan than never talking about it because it's too awkward or uncomfortable. Just hoping for the best rarely turns out well," said Maya.

"Spoken like a true contract lawyer," said her husband.

"Don't the French have a term for that?" asked Rose. "*C'est la vie?*"

"That might be how I thought about our finances," admitted Joe. "At least before we took this cruise."

"No more!" said Betty. "We're going to have some long talks and do some solid planning. I'm going to put at least as much prep into my retirement as I do into my curriculum."

"But not tonight," said Rose. "Tonight, I want to go see the floor show. It's supposed to be based on dancers at the Moulin Rouge."

"Cancan girls?" her husband teased. "Count me in!"

Chapter Seven

ENJOY THE LIFE YOU HAVE

The Morning Ritual

That morning, both the men and the women decided to get up early and walk around the top deck of the ship. Although they normally split up, with the women in one group and the men in another, today they found themselves splitting off into different pairings. While Gabriela, Peter, and Rose discussed the stresses of running a business, Lamont found himself walking with Shirley.

"Don't feel like talking shop this morning?" he asked her. "The other business owners are happily comparing accounting methods and how to cut through red tape."

Shirley laughed. "It's too early in the morning for me to talk about red tape," she told Lamont. "And if I never talk about accounting methods, I would be a very happy camper."

Lamont smiled in agreement. "I keep it simple. I send invoices, people pay me, I keep a spreadsheet. My wife has employees and overhead, but I'm a sole proprietor who works from home—a one-man band. Self-employment tax is the one thorn in my side; other than trying to remember to send those checks to the government on time, I don't stress too much."

"You know, I really admire you," Shirley told him. "You get to do what you want for a living."

"Don't you?"

Shirley shrugged. "The store has been a part of my life for so long, it feels like home. And it was perfect when the kids were small. It allowed me to combine work and motherhood in a way I never could have if I'd been working for someone else. But I never had a passion for running a business, certainly not the way your wife has."

"Gabriela has the heart of an entrepreneur," Lamont agreed. "She loves to solve problems. She rarely gets frustrated when things go wrong. Instead, she's energized by it ruining her business. If it looks impossible to overcome, she's even happier."

Shirley shook her head. "That is definitely not me!" She looked out at the water sparkling in the early morning sunshine. "I envy you your talent. It must be wonderful to be able to capture an image with your paintbrush. And to do that for a living!"

"Most of the freelance work I do is as a graphic designer," Lamont said. "It's pretty much like any nine-to-five, although I do appreciate that I get to work in the visual arts. I would not be happy selling insurance, which is what my father did for thirty years. But I'd love to do more of my own creative work. That's the dream!"

"I want to write," Shirley confided.

Lamont looked intrigued. "Really? What kinds of things?"

"Everything," she said. "I've got three children's books sitting in a drawer, as well as a half-finished novel. I've also been thinking about a line of greeting cards for the modern age. Young people tend to text or email—you need something really special to get them to pick up a pen and actually write a card. They're not really going to send each other birthday cards the way we did, but they will send them to their grandparents, for instance. And they need cards for weddings and baby showers and thank-yous, but they want messages and images that feel fun and fresh, you know what I mean?"

"As a graphic designer, I know exactly what you mean," Lamont said. "Connecting with the younger demographic is always at the top of the client's list. So how much have you developed this greeting card idea?"

"Quite a bit," Shirley admitted. "Obviously, I have a lot of experience selling greeting cards, and it gets a bit frustrating not being able to find something I know I could sell. I've been paying attention for the last couple of years to what people say they're looking for and what they actually buy—and what they pick up, read, and put down again. And it's been fun to try my hand at writing a few. But I wouldn't know how to sell my ideas even if I put a portfolio together."

"Why would you have to sell the idea to someone else?" Lamont asked. "You own a card store. Sounds to me like you have the potential for a great side business, selling directly to the public."

"Do you think so?"

"Absolutely. And," Lamont added, "if you need an artist to illustrate the cards, I'd love to apply for the job."

Shirley stopped in her tracks. "Are you kidding me?" she asked.

"Not at all," he said. "I've been looking for a way to be more creative and to get my own work out in the world. We'd have to hammer out what the partnership would look like—one of the things that would matter to me would be a certain amount of creative control. I already spend most of my time making other people's visions come to life. I'm looking for a way to make my own vision happen. But it sounds like you've done a lot of market research. You have a new and different approach to an established product. And you have built-in distribution to see if there's really a customer base with very little risk. What's not to like about the project?" Lamont smiled. "If you're game, I'd love to work with you."

Slowly, Shirley nodded. "I need to think about it," she said, because suddenly what had been more of a daydream was starting to become very real.

"Hey, slowpokes!" called Sam. "Hurry up! I'm ready for breakfast."

"But are you ready for your wife to launch her own line of greeting cards?" Shirley called back.

"Finally!" Sam grinned. "I've been telling her for years what a brilliant idea it is." He took his wife's hand as she and Lamont joined him. "Besides, we're going to need extra income to fund more cruises. I'm hooked!"

Reality Check: Rose and Peter

After breakfast, the couples drifted apart. Peter and Rose headed to Gunnar's office. They were excited to have their session with him and arrived with time to spare. Gunnar rose to meet them.

"Early birds!" he said. "My kind of people."

"Don't kid yourself," Rose laughed as her husband helped her into a chair. "We're only early because it takes me so long to get anywhere lately, we have to plan extra time. Some days, like today, I'm less creaky than others."

Gunnar grinned. "That makes you even more my type of people. You gave yourself resources—in this case, time—to make sure that everything would go smoothly. That is the essence of planning for retirement. You two don't need me—you already have the right mindset!"

"Why don't we tell you our situation anyway?" Peter smiled. "I think we would welcome your expertise."

Peter set a folder on the table. In it, the couple had put together their financial picture. Gunnar, delighted, looked over the numbers.

"My grandfather and his brother started a lumber mill in Washington State," Peter began. "My mother inherited part of it, and she and my dad eventually bought out her cousins, neither of whom wanted to run a lumber mill or even stay in the Pacific Northwest. I grew up watching my parents run the business, and it was always what I wanted to do as well. I took over from them when they retired, and Rose and I have run it much like my parents did."

"Our son is a doctor, however," Rose said. "He has no interest in the lumber mill at all, and there isn't anyone else in the family who would want to take it over."

"Are you considering selling the business?"

"Absolutely," answered Peter. "We have a buyer lined up. The deal is worth $8 million, and we expect to clear $5 million after taxes and expenses related to the sale."

"I don't want to sell our house, though," Rose cut in. "Even if our son, Sean, doesn't want it, there are so many memories there that I'm not ready to let go of."

"The mortgage is paid on it," Peter added, "so it's not a burden."

"And you have to live somewhere," Gunnar added.

"Yes, although we're hoping to travel quite a bit over the next year," Rose said. "This is really what we want to talk to you about. I'm a breast cancer survivor; it's one of the things that inspired Sean to become an oncologist. My cancer has returned," she told him frankly, "and while I am trying everything available to fight it, I don't know how much time I have left. I'd like to see more of the world before I go, and I especially want to organize a family trip with Sean and his wife and two children, so that we have some lovely memories of all of us together."

Gunnar nodded. "That's one of the great gifts financial planning offers us: the chance to do what we want with the time that we have. Let's take a look at the numbers, shall we?"

> Rose and Peter Li are both in their early seventies. Although Peter is healthy and physically fit for his age, Rose is battling cancer. She also has a heart murmur and tires easily. They have one son, a doctor, and no one else in the family who would want to take over the family lumber mill, inherited by Peter from his parents. They have lined up an outside buyer for the mill.

> Rose helped run the business side of the mill and raised their son, surviving an early bout of cancer that has now recurred. As an oncologist and research specialist in the cancer field, their son is doing well financially; they were able to help him with his medical education so that he's not weighed down by student loans. He's married to a fellow research scientist and they have two children.

For Peter and Rose, their primary concern isn't necessarily retention of wealth. In the short term, at least, they want to enjoy life to the fullest while Rose is still physically able to travel. In addition, Rose would like to set up a trust for her grandchildren's education. Their lifestyle requires $300K a year to maintain, and Gunnar suggests increasing that amount to $500K for the coming year to cover the additional travel and entertaining that Peter and Rose hope to do.

Peter and Rose have a joint savings and checking account totaling $50,000.

They own their home outright; it's worth $800,000.

They have no pensions, but both have Roth IRA accounts, primarily invested in index funds, with a combined total of $400K.

In addition, they are on the verge of selling their business for a net gain of $5 million.

Gunnar's recommendations:

Set aside $1M of the sale money: $500K for contingencies and $500K to set up an irrevocable family trust for their grandchildren. The contingency funds should be in accounts that are fairly liquid—in other words, easy to access.

Increase the money in their savings account to $150K and put the rest into a combination of short- and medium-term certificates of deposit, treasury bills, and treasury bonds.

Establish an investment trust with the remaining $4M

from the sale for their retirement income. In a diverse portfolio investment, and once again assuming a 3 percent rate of inflation, it would operate as follows:

INTEREST RATE ON ANNUAL INCOME OF $204,077	VALUE WITH 3% INFLATION RATE OVER 30 YEARS
6%	$204,077
8%	$260,205
10%	$322,345

Take money from their IRAs for the extra expenses they're planning for this coming year. Even if they take only $204K from their retirement trust, they'll have enough extra money from their IRAs that they'll be able to splurge on traveling with their entire family without touching the money they'd set aside for emergencies.

Gunnar studied the couple as they reviewed their Reality Check numbers and his recommendations. He considered his proposal very conservative. Historically, the stock market has gone up at least 10 percent annually over the long haul.

"Of course you should speak to your lawyers," he said. "I am not qualified to give you specific legal advice.

"As to the irrevocable trust, I can tell you the upside to such a decision: An irrevocable trust does not count toward the value of your estate. You can't change your mind later—that's the big difference between revocable and irrevocable trusts—but since you both are agreed that you want this money to go to your grandchildren, that's not really an issue here."

In addition, Gunnar suggested they discuss philanthropy. What were their priorities? What charities or nonprofits did work that they believed in and wanted to be part of?

"It's always important to think about what impact we want to have on the world," Gunnar told them. "Not just in terms of legacy, but also because after retirement, we want to do things that keep us involved in the world; we want to see ourselves as living for a greater purpose. Many people take up charity work to fill the time, and that's great, but doing it with intention, making sure your money and your time are aligned with your vision for a better world—that gives you the most impact on the issues you care about as well as on your life. For instance, I know your son works for a nonprofit cancer research center. You might want to talk to the center about what kind of a trust you might set up or gift you might want to give that would help them while at the same time offering you tax advantages. And you would be making a positive difference in the world."

Finally, Gunnar encouraged Peter and Rose to start planning their family trip immediately. "You have the cash flow," he said, "and you have a strong desire. Why put it off? And planning a vacation or other event that you're really looking forward to only increases the enjoyment. You get to anticipate the experience; it's almost like getting to experience it twice. And there really is no time like the present to start enjoying your life."

WHO KNOWS WHERE THE CHECKBOOK IS?

While Rose and Peter were having their session with Gunnar, Rachael met up with the other women in the piano bar.

"What's the topic for today?" Maya asked.

"I want to conquer the stock market," said Gabriela. "When is that on the menu?"

"William will definitely be talking more about stocks and bonds before the trip is out," Rachael promised. "But I have an equally important question for you: In your house, who knows where the checkbook is—or the login information to your back account?"

The women looked at her in surprise.

"I do," said Betty. "I pay our bills."

Most of the women nodded in agreement. Gabriela, however, frowned.

"I think I do . . ." she said. "It's Lamont who handles our household bills. I'm pretty sure the checkbook lives in the top drawer of his desk."

"What about your husbands?" Rachael asked the others. "We'll assume Lamont knows for sure where it is, since he pays the bills, but what about the rest of the men?"

"Sam definitely has no idea," Shirley said. "Every time he wants to write a check, he asks me where it is. Which is silly, because it hasn't moved in twenty years."

"Joe knows," Betty said. "We keep our checks and spending cash in a box in our bedroom. He sees the checkbook every time he needs to refill his wallet. He'd better know it's there by now!"

"I don't think Andrei knows," Maya said thoughtfully. "He keeps the books for his business and of course he has a separate checking account for that, but I can't remember the last time he wrote a check from our account."

"This is what I want to talk to you about today," said Rachael. "It's not the checkbook; it's the fact that in very few households do both partners know where the checkbook is. Or where the fuse box is. Or where your passports are, or the key to the safe deposit box, or the phone numbers for the babysitter and the pediatrician.

"Sometimes one person—and traditionally, that has been the man—will take care of car maintenance for both of you. I once helped a woman put gas in her car; she was in her seventies and had just lost her husband, who had always been the one to fill the tank. 'Don't do it for me,' she said. 'Show me how to do it myself.' I did, and I've never forgotten it.

"It's critical for both partners to know where important papers are kept and where the fuse box is, things like that. We naturally split tasks when we are in a relationship, there's nothing wrong with that. But you want to make sure that if one of you suddenly had to go to the hospital, for instance, the other one would be able to have whatever they needed to keep the home fires burning."

"How do you suggest we do that?" Betty asked. "I don't even know what I know that Joe doesn't."

"Well, there's always trial by fire," Rachael said. "You could wait until there's an emergency and see how it goes. I don't recommend that."

"No," Shirley agreed. "That sounds like a recipe for disaster."

"So maybe start by each of you writing down all the things you can think of that you alone do. Making doctor's appointments, for instance, or changing lightbulbs. Focus on what you *do* know, not on what you *don't* know. Start by just writing the thing itself down. And then, when you have a pretty good list, start adding information to it. What are the important phone numbers? Where is the title to the car? If it's something that's done on a regular basis, start giving instructions. How do you change the filter in the refrigerator? What's the schedule for draining the water heater? And then share your lists with each other.

"Take this opportunity to go through your files as well. Make sure things are well marked and important papers are easy to find. Make binders with prompts for what your family should know if something should happen to you. It's very useful for each of you to fill those out and keep them someplace obvious. It focuses mostly on your financial picture, but there's often room for personalization, and the prompts are indispensable."

"It feels a little morbid to fill one of those out," said Maya.

"Not if you tell yourself it's in case you decide to spend six months on a world cruise!" Gabriela laughed.

"That's an excellent idea!" Rachael agreed. "One thing you may discover is that neither of you knows where some things are, and it's definitely time well spent finding, say, your life insurance policies or your social security cards before you need them."

"This is like the emergency drills when we first came on board, isn't it?" Shirley asked.

"Exactly," answered Rachael. "Hope you'll never need them, but be sure you know where those lifeboats are!"

LECTURE 6: ANNUITIES

William waited for everyone to be seated. "Today," he told them, "I want to follow up our discussions of recession and inflation and even cycles by talking about the emotions you may have felt after those lectures. No, this isn't about to turn into an emotional support group, but I do want you to recognize that you make your financial decisions based on emotion as much as—or sometimes even more than—logic. And thinking about recessions and inflation and the uncertainty of cycles might make you uncomfortable, and that, in turn, can make you look for ways to feel secure in your finances. I want to tell you a story that shows the possibilities and the pitfalls of seeking security."

He motioned for the house lights to be lowered and clicked the remote to turn on the projector. A couple appeared onscreen, standing behind a young woman with Down syndrome.

"Fred and Kathy came on this tour a year ago. They enjoyed the international cuisine, the ports of call, and, I hope, these workshops. They sat down with Gunnar and, for the most part, their retirement plan was solid. Fred was fifty-nine and was planning to work for another six years, while Kathy was sixty-two and retired. She was receiving Social Security, but Kathy's primary focus, and the thing that had kept her from working more than part-time most of her career, was their daughter, Maria, who has Down syndrome. Kathy pivoted in her publishing career after Maria was born, giving up her full-time job to work as a freelance editor and care for Maria at home. Maria is twenty-seven, is in good health, and can do many things on her own. But with Down syndrome, as with everything else, there is a wide range of abilities, and Maria falls on the end where she is unable to hold down a job. She continues to live with her parents at home and receives an SSI monthly check for almost $700 to cover some of her expenses.

"Kathy and Fred have managed pretty well. They also have a son who does not have Down syndrome, and they were able to put him through college so that he has been able to start off his adult life unburdened with student debt. Kathy made enough in her freelance business that she is eligible for Social Security, and she and Fred have set aside some money for retirement. Nothing lavish, but their needs are met."

William clicked through some slides, showing a modest but well-maintained house in a small Pennsylvania town and a family who looked content.

"I promised you a conversation about finances and emotions, and here it is: Kathy and Fred were worried about Maria. Their son, three years younger than his sister, was doing fine, but was at the very beginning of his own career. The couple had taken out term life insurance when Maria was born, but that had run its twenty-five-year term. That's the downside of term insurance: It's often all you can afford when you're young and need significant amounts of life insurance, but unlike whole life insurance, it doesn't last your entire life—and life insurance gets even more expensive, if not impossible to get, as you age. What if something happened to them? How would Maria be taken care of? In the midst of uncertainty, Kathy and Fred longed for security.

"I've never really talked much about annuities; I just mentioned them along with bonds as a conservative investment. But it was enough to get them thinking, and when they went home after their cruise, Fred found an annuity broker. They made an appointment to go over their concerns.

"The broker—we won't use his real name, I'll call him Louis—explained that the first consideration when buying an annuity is to determine its purpose. He asked Kathy and Fred to list their priorities and gave them some examples of what he considered the upside of annuities: security, guaranteed income, protection from market trends, protection from creditors, some tax implications, and—depending on what kind of annuity they chose—the possibility of a death benefit or the ability to liquidate the annuity in case of special need. These things are not guaranteed with every annuity, by the way. There are different types of annuities, some of which have more risk than others. You should never, ever enter into an annuity if you don't fully understand the fine print. But no matter what kind of annuity you get, at heart, an annuity is a contract between you and an insurance company.

"Essentially, you give the insurance company a chunk of money and they promise to give you a small slice of it back every month for as long as you live. Now, the question is: Why would you do that? How is that better than keeping the money in the bank or in a box under your bed? There are some tax implications, but really the value is in two things. The first is a gamble; the second is security. Here's what the gamble looks like: You are betting that you will live longer than the insurance company thinks you will. And, to put it bluntly, they are betting that you'll die.

"Let's use some made-up numbers to keep it simple, so you can see what I mean. Let's say you give the insurance company $100,000, and in exchange, they promise to give you $500 a month for the rest of your life. You would have to live 200 months to break even, or roughly sixteen and a half years. If you live twenty more years, that's good for you, bad for the insurance company; they will have had to pay out an extra $21,000. On the other hand, if you only live ten years, they pocket the $39,000 left over from your $100,000 investment. A pretty simple gamble, right? One I hope you would all win, but remember that insurance companies have a lot of data about how long people live—that is their wheelhouse. You know what I think about gambling: The house always has the odds in their favor.

"But the reason the gamble is enticing is really the emotions around both investing and growing older. So much is out of our control. What we long for—and what we're willing to pay for—is certainty. With an annuity, you are paying for the peace of mind of knowing that you will get that $500—or whatever, these are made-up numbers for ease of explanation—every month for as long as you live. Market up, market down, no matter. That $500 can be counted on."

William paused for a drink of water. He smiled out at the audience. "Let's do a quick reality check of our own, though, right? Not every company can be counted on. Your annuity is only as secure as the insurance backing it. You have to be very careful when choosing an annuity that the company will still be there in twenty or thirty years. And many people don't think of inflation as a factor. That $500 a month will inevitably have less purchasing power in twenty years than it does today. The security you think will be there is an illusion.

"Let's take another look at the $100,000 investment. If you put $100K in an index fund, you could conservatively expect to make 6 percent a year every year. Which means in ten years, your $100K investment would have almost doubled in ten years, thanks to compound interest, to $180K. 'But,' you say to me, 'that's only if I don't touch the money. What about that $500 a month that I want to take out?' Let's go ahead and run the numbers."

William put up a new slide. This one showed what would happen if $500 per month was taken out of the $100K investment.

"Five hundred dollars a month adds up to $6,000 every year. Investing $100K in an index fund that generates 6 percent interest each year gives you $6,000 in interest. Which means that taking out $500 every month for ten years or twenty years or a hundred years still leaves you with your entire $100K investment intact."

He paused to look around at the faces in the auditorium as his audience absorbed the implications.

"And this is where the house always wins," he told them. "That insurance company isn't plunking your money in a box and pulling $500 a month out of it to send to you. They are investing it themselves! Which means they, too, never really run out of money to send you no matter how long you live. And I haven't even begun to talk about how expensive annuities can be in terms of fees and other costs," he added. "There's actually a saying in the financial world: 'Annuities aren't bought, they're sold.' Meaning that the value in an annuity is in how the seller spins it, not in the financial product itself. And spin it they will, because annuities pay big commissions to the brokers who sell them.

"I'm not saying some of you won't decide to buy annuities because of the second value they provide, the feeling of security. It may be an illusion, as I hope I've shown you, but it's powerful nonetheless. There is something very seductive about security. Our brains want that comfort more than anything else. Just remember that markets go up and they go down, sure, but in the long run, they pretty much only go up. You need to have resources so that you're not forced to sell when the market is low, but once you have that—again, that emergency cash reserve should be the first thing each of you gets in place when you go home—you're pretty much freed from worrying about volatility. That's true security, and that's what I want for you."

William clicked the remote and another slide came up. It showed a slightly older Fred and Kathy with their daughter and son.

"To come full circle, Fred and Kathy looked at their priorities, which were to make sure their daughter was taken care of after they were gone, and that she would have a guaranteed income that could keep up with inflation. They were savvy enough after taking this cruise that they could run the numbers and see what made sense and what didn't. And ultimately, they decided the annuity that the broker, Louis, offered didn't make sense to them.

"He suggested investing a major chunk of their retirement savings, which included an inheritance from Kathy's mother, totaling $400,000, into an annuity that only paid out $6,000 a year, because Maria was so young. It meant Maria would have to live to be in her nineties just to break even—and over sixty-six years, think how much less purchasing power that $6K a year would have. They were also concerned about what would happen if they suddenly needed the money; there were significant penalties for pulling out of the contract. Louis tried to talk to them about how the stock market was unpredictable and that they were risking a huge loss by keeping the money in the stock market, but Kathy countered with the fact that while stocks may decrease in the short term, if you look over the course of decades, the market has consistently gone up.

"Fred ran some numbers, showing that at 6 percent compound interest, their $400K investment would double in only twelve years. They could pull out $6,000 a year for Maria, and over the next fifty years, their initial $400,000 would grow to over $5 million. Now that's how you make sure your daughter has a guaranteed income that keeps up with inflation. Ultimately, they decided against an annuity and instead set up a trust for both their children, investing that same $400K in an index fund and naming their son as a successor trustee should anything happen to them. Maria's needs would be taken care of during her lifetime, and their son's children would ultimately inherit the balance of the funds."

William turned off the projector and the lights came back up. "I don't want to give anyone specific advice about which financial products are right for them, and that includes trusts versus annuities, or individual stocks versus index funds. But I do want to give you examples and tools to allow you to evaluate for yourselves what you're being offered.

"Above all, I want you to realize that 'certainty' and 'security' are words that make us feel good, that calm our fears, but they come at a very steep price. I personally believe that real security comes from having a diversified portfolio, investing in yourself, and having enough cash on hand that you don't fall prey to letting fear make decisions for you—decisions that will lead you to sell low, or to not take any risks in the first place. Because a fixed income isn't really fixed: It only ever loses purchasing power. Playing it safe can come at a tremendous cost."

Shore Leave: St. Francisville

As Shirley was getting ready to leave for their tour of St. Francisville, she noticed that Sam was more thoughtful than usual. "You're awfully quiet," she told him. "You feeling okay?"

"I'm fine," Sam answered. "It's just—William has talked about inflation a few times now, and that's the one thing I'm really worried about. I was thinking about Germany, and my granddad telling horror stories of what the German people faced after the First World War. Germany had to pay so much in reparations to other countries for the destruction caused by the war that they just started printing marks like mad. Marks became worthless. Prices rose so fast that the price of bread would become unaffordable within a day; a gold mark was worth one paper mark in 1918, and worth 1 *trillion* marks only five years later. How can we be sure we'll have enough in retirement if inflation threatens to devalue everything we've saved?"

Shirley took a moment to respond. "It's true that inflation is always a danger. But unlike post-World War I Germany, we do have an economy that's pretty stable. I don't think we can look at the worst possible scenario and catastrophize—and I don't think William would want us to. What we can do," she added, "is come up with a plan to make the most of what we have, now and even after retirement. The duplex, for instance. And the store. And Lamont and I are talking about collaborating on a line of greeting cards. I think the most important thing we've learned on this cruise is that we do have options. There's always something we can do to make the situation better. Worrying doesn't help."

Sam nodded. "You're right," he said. "This is not the time to give up. Catastrophic inflation isn't happening yet. And because of this cruise we're much better positioned to handle it if it does, or if something else crazy happens."

"Yes!" agreed Shirley. "We are much better prepared than we were a week ago. Now hop to it—I don't want to miss the bus into St. Francisville."

The two of them met up with Gabriela and Lamont to take the tour to Oakley Plantation. Lamont was especially excited about the tour because they would get to see where the artist John James Audubon painted many of his famous bird studies.

"Now this was an artist with a vision," Lamont explained to Gabriela, Shirley, and Sam as they got off the tour bus at Oakley Plantation. "Audubon wanted to paint every bird in North America and ended up discovering some new species while he was at it. And nothing stopped him, not rats eating his pictures, not going bankrupt, not getting tossed into debtor's prison . . . ."

His wife stopped him there. "I love that you love his enthusiasm," she said, "but don't feel the need to go that far to prove you're just as good an artist!"

Lamont laughed. "I'm a different kind of artist, obviously, but I do admire his tenacity. What I think is interesting is how Audubon combined art and science in a way that really spoke to people. He opened us up to the beauty of nature. What a legacy to have given the world."

"It says here that he came to Oakley to teach painting," said Shirley, reading the museum guide. "And then he spent his free time roaming the grounds painting birds. He also wandered the country as an itinerant portrait painter."

"Meanwhile, his wife was the family breadwinner," noted Sam. "What was it that William was talking about? Having multiple streams of income?"

"I think families have always banded together to help each other succeed," Gabriela said, "although it's probably better to do it deliberately by planning to have multiple income streams rather than suddenly having to scramble when the income you were counting on dries up. I know Lamont and I are a team. When I was just starting my business, he supported us by working in advertising. Once my business took off, he was able to quit his full-time job and start his freelancing business."

Lamont affectionately squeezed his wife's hand.

While the others were touring Oakley, Betty and Joe decided to check out the Myrtles Plantation.

"They say it's haunted," said Betty, reading the brochure.

"In that case," answered her husband, "I vote we keep to the gardens."

"Actually, the gardens have their own ghost," Betty began, only to realize Joe had wandered off to look at the pond. It was large enough to have a small island in the middle of it.

With a laugh, Betty caught up with him and took his arm. As they toured the grounds, she was surprised to see Joe so excited about the beautiful landscaping and gardens.

"What's gotten into you?" she asked. "I've never seen you so interested in the great outdoors unless you had a fishing pole with you!"

"I've been thinking about what I want to do now that I'm retired," Joe admitted. "Now that the kids are gone, I thought I'd turn the backyard into a garden."

Betty was taken by surprise. "What kind of garden?"

Joe shrugged. "Mainly vegetables. Lettuce, tomatoes, peppers, that kind of thing. Lots of herbs for cooking."

"Well, if you're looking for support from me, you have it. I would love to cook with fresh herbs from the garden!"

"I don't know if I'll be any good at it," Joe said. "And it's certainly not going to make us any income. I'm not looking to farm our acre and a half, just to putter around and grow a few things that we'll enjoy."

"Joe, a kitchen garden is a great idea," Betty told him firmly. "Not everything in life has to translate into a moneymaking scheme. We need to enjoy life as we go. I think you having something new to learn and do is a terrific way to start off your retirement. It'll keep you sharp and keep you from turning into a couch potato. I wish my dad had found a new hobby when he retired. I think it would have improved his health no end to go out and dig some holes in the backyard."

"I'm planning to build raised beds. Put my carpentry skills to good use."

"Even better! Just be sure to plant a few flowers. It'll help bring in bees to pollinate, and I'll get to have fresh flowers on my dinner table as well as fresh veggies."

Joe smiled. "You've got a deal."

LECTURE 7: REGULATORY CONTROLS

That evening, the passengers discovered they had a choice for dinner. Many couples chose to eat in the main dining hall, but others opted for sandwiches and soda in the lounge while William gave a bonus lecture on regulatory controls. Rose wasn't feeling up to another lecture, so she and Peter decided on a hot meal and an early night, but the other couples grabbed one of the tables that had been set up in the lounge. They helped themselves to food and drink and settled in to listen.

There was a single chair on the small stage where the band usually performed. William glanced around the room as he entered and took his seat.

"No PowerPoint today," he laughed. "No slides, just me. And sandwiches. You all are devoted to learning this stuff—congratulations. Today, we're going to talk about the regulatory controls that influence our economy. They smooth over the rough times and the aberrations, everything from recessions to inflation to outright fraud. Because unfortunately, as long as there are people involved in making money, there will be people involved in conning you out of your money. You have only to look at the headlines: Theranos, Enron, Bernie Madoff.

"To go back a bit, there was a case in the 1980s where a guy named Barry Minkow and his team created over 20,000 fake documents, leased a multimillion-dollar office complex, and went public with a phony business that ended up being worth about $200 million before it all came tumbling down. The kicker? Minkow was sixteen years old when he founded the company, nineteen when it went public, and just twenty-two when he was convicted of fraud for the first time. I always shake my head when I see how much hard work people put into committing fraud. If folks would put that much effort into creating something of real value, the world would be a much better place.

"But I'm not telling you these stories to scare you," William continued. "Rather, I want you to understand that there have always been and will always be bad actors. Just like recessions and inflation and so many other things we can't control, we need to assume that fraud is always possible and not put all our eggs in one basket. Diversification, multiple sources of income, insurance—these are all steps you can take to protect yourself no matter what the market or individual companies or con artists might do. And, in addition to protecting yourself, there are regulatory agencies whose job is to protect you. This isn't meant to be exhaustive, but I do want to give you an overview.

"First, there is the United States Treasury. You may have heard of it." William smiled as a few people chuckled. "The UST was founded during the American Revolution. In fact, it predates the Declaration of Independence. The nascent country needed a way to fund itself; then, as now, the country needed someone to manage federal financing. After the war, the Treasury became a full-fledged governmental department. The first secretary of the Treasury was a young guy called Alexander Hamilton. Despite the musical that bears his name, I don't know if Hamilton himself could carry a tune, but he did know an awful lot about finance. His leadership laid the foundation for the new country's economic stability.

"Over the years, the Department of the Treasury has grown with the country, continually taking on new responsibilities as the economy has become more complex. At one point, it oversaw programs as diverse as the Coast Guard and the Bureau of Narcotics, although both of those have since been moved to other departments. It continues to oversee a wide variety of bureaus, including the Alcohol and Tobacco Tax and Trade Bureau; the Bureau of Engraving and Printing, which creates the currency in your wallet; the Financial Crimes Enforcement Network, which combats money laundering, among other crimes; and the Internal Revenue Service, which needs no introduction.

"For this discussion, I want to go into a little depth on two bureaus that fall under the purview of the Treasury Department. The first is the

Office of the Comptroller of the Currency. According to their website, this office 'charters, regulates, and supervises all national banks and federal savings associations.' It was established under Abraham Lincoln in part to create a system of national banks and a uniform national currency. We take this for granted today, and in fact our country could not function without it, but at the time, different local banks created different paper money. It was chaotic, and worse, subject to rampant counterfeiting, which eroded public trust. Having a national banking system and uniform currency created confidence and a sense of unity. This is a lesson from history, but it shows you the way in which governmental regulation can serve the best interests of the people.

"The second bureau I want to discuss is the IRS. The IRS is responsible for the collection of taxes and enforcement of tax laws. We joke about tax collectors, but the IRS takes great pride in their efficiency, processing over 240 million tax returns a year, and in enforcing the tax laws with integrity. They oversee the taxes not just of individuals, but also of corporations and estates, as well as employment, gift, and excise taxes. One of the amazing things within the system of collecting taxes in our country is the trust given to taxpayers to prepare their own tax liability. Sure, there are audits, but nonetheless, much of our taxes are paid on what is essentially an honor system.

"By the way, while the IRS looks into tax fraud, the Securities and Exchange Commission looks after the stock market. They have a three-pronged mission: to protect investors, to keep the markets safe and fair, and to help develop capital. It grew out of the stock market crash of 1929 with the extraordinary idea that, hey, companies selling stock should try not to hoodwink investors. Teenage Barry Minkow didn't get that memo, mind you, but he did serve time thanks to some of the checks and balances that were put into place with this regulatory agency."

William paused and took a sip of water. It gave everyone a minute to think about how much more precarious their investments would be without the regulations that had been put in place.

"Okay," William continued, "on to the Federal Reserve Board. It is regarded as one of the most powerful economic institutions in the United States. The Federal Reserve chair is nominated by the president and confirmed by the Senate. And the tenures tend to be long ones, for stability's sake. You've probably heard of Alan Greenspan, who held the position for over eighteen years.

"The Federal Reserve is the country's central bank and is responsible for maintaining, per its website, 'a safe, flexible, and stable monetary and financial system.' What does that look like? It's actually a wide range of responsibilities, from conducting monetary policy to minimize risk and encourage employment to controlling the interest rate to slow down or heat up the economy. It also includes monitoring banks, fostering community development, and providing consumer protection. They pretty much have their hand in every economic pie, and they need to, because the Federal Reserve's key role is in preventing a financial crisis—things like bank failures, panics, and credit scarcity. Their goal is to serve the public interest, and they analyze information from multiple sources on an ongoing basis to try to keep up with the economic trends.

"You have to understand, the sands of our economy are constantly shifting under so many different influences. There's the demand for natural resources, changing labor needs, fluctuating demands for products and services. And we are part of a global economy as well, which means we need to factor in hard currencies, which tend to be stable and hold their value, and soft currencies, which aren't and don't. Political and social pressures both domestic and foreign can provide pressure that might unbalance our economy. We need to be able to count on the Federal Reserve to rebalance things and correct the economic situation.

"Speaking of the global economy, let's talk about the Bretton Woods Agreement. In 1944, after World War II, the Allied nations got together and essentially agreed to cooperate economically to avoid trade wars and keep their currencies stable against the United States' dollar. This was a shift from before the war, when governments pinned their currencies to gold. But at the time, the U.S. held three-quarters of the world's gold. Pinning their currencies to the dollar instead of to gold gave postwar countries some necessary flexibility while combating hyperinflation. The agreement also created the World Bank and the International Monetary Fund. The World Bank's mission has shifted over the years, from helping rebuild Europe after the second World

War to, today, reducing poverty by investing in emerging economies. These agencies also have 'tools' in their toolboxes to help monitor the world's economic equilibrium.

"So why am I devoting an entire dinner to this? And, by the way, I hope you enjoyed the sandwiches. It breaks Chef Luigi's heart when I take you away from his dining room, but he tries to make up for it in the variety and excellence of his sandwich spread. So why am I depriving you of a hot meal and making Luigi's life difficult? Because I want you to understand two things.

"First, our economy is an ecosystem. It requires checks and balances to protect investors from devastating losses, as global as the 1929 crash or as localized, but equally tragic, as the shareholders who collectively lost hundreds of millions of dollars at the hands of people like Minkow. You don't want it to be the Wild West, not when your pension and quality of life are on the line.

"Second, I want you to recognize how very many factors are at play. It is virtually impossible to accurately predict what the economy will do; by the time we realize we are headed in one direction, it has already happened. The only forecasters who have it 'right' are those looking in the rearview mirror. All forward projections are no more than educated guesses. Will they be right? Some of the time, yes. Other times, no. True economic experts understand this. Friedrich von Hayek understood this when he won the Nobel Prize in Economics. He titled his speech 'The Pretense of Knowledge,' and for good reason. In the economic world, anything can happen—and does, almost daily. No one has a crystal ball, and anyone trying to convince you that they do, that they have all the answers on where you should invest your money, is lying.

"This is why it's so important to diversify your holdings, keep some reserves in cash and bonds even if they won't grow the way a stock portfolio can grow. What goes up will probably someday go down—and if it happens to be a day when you really need that money, you find yourself forced into selling at the low end of the market, and that, to me, is tragic. Take risks, yes, but understand exactly what risks you're taking. Recognize which organizations are there to watch your financial back. Understand what factors are at play and how the economy and the markets all depend on a multiplicity of factors, some of which we have no control over. Be in the game so you can enjoy the highs, but mitigate your risk with holdings that will let you ride out the lows."

With this, William wrapped up his presentation. The servers brought out plates of chocolate chip cookies and urns of coffee, and the couples found themselves thinking over his lecture in companionable silence before turning in for an early night.

Chapter Eight

AN ABUNDANCE OF OPTIONS

The Morning Ritual

The entire group met up for an on-the-go breakfast, walking the promenade deck with coffee and muffins while discussing William's points. They wanted to make sure Peter and Rose got the full benefit, but they also found themselves feeling a little low after the lecture.

"There's just so much to take in," Sam said, putting into words what most of them were feeling. "I mean, between the competing forces of labor and management, supply and demand, even the constant train of new technology barreling down on us . . . ."

"It's a wonder we have any economy at all," his wife added, "much less one as stable as we do."

"History has shown that we tend to run to extremes," Betty mused. "That train you mentioned, Sam—it's not just technology. It's people seeing some new trend pulling out of the station and jumping on it so fast they don't even realize where the train is going until they're halfway there. If we didn't have some regulations in place, the whole thing would probably crash every couple of decades."

"As a business owner," said Andrei, "I've never been a fan of regulations. But I have to admit, I prefer it when the train and the economy both stay on track."

"I heard that last night was a run-up to William talking about investing in the stock market," Gabriela said. "That's one lecture I'm really looking forward to hearing."

"Well, if his goal was to sober us up so we don't jump on the first IPO train we see coming," her husband laughed, "he did a great job."

"Balance is what he wants us to pay attention to," Joe said. "I think that's smart. Too many people want you to get carried away and invest without thinking things through first. I think Lamont's right—last night was the ballast to counter our excitement about getting into the stock market."

"I'll tell you what I'm excited to get into," Rose said. "And that's the sauna. I'm really looking forward to our spa day this afternoon."

"We'd better head back down," Maya told her husband. "It's nearly time for our Reality Check with Gunnar."

"Good luck!" said Shirley. "It was certainly eye-opening for us."

"I wish we had done it when we were your age," Joe added. "Betty and I would have more options now if we'd thought about it sooner."

"Oh, I don't know, Joe," said his wife. "One of the reassuring things about this cruise has been realizing that we're all doing the best we can, and that there are always opportunities to do better, no matter where you are. We'll be able to figure this out. Besides," she added with a smile, "you're going to grow some prizewinning tomatoes and we'll be the talk of the town!"

Joe laughed. Everyone wished Maya and Andrei well as they set off to meet with Gunnar.

Reality Check: Maya and Andrei

Gunnar was waiting for the couple in his office. He smiled as they walked in.

"It's so heartening to see young people on these cruises," he said. "Time is your most important asset, and it's exciting to see you taking advantage of it."

132

Maya laughed. "I don't know how young we are!"

"It's not the years, it's the sleepless nights," Andrei quipped. "Two young kids and a startup don't leave much time for anything else."

"I still say you're ahead of the game," Gunnar told them. "And I want to talk to you about playing it at a higher level."

Andrei and Maya are both in their mid-thirties. Their oldest child is just starting school and the younger one will be going to morning preschool starting soon after they return from the cruise.

Andrei has a startup business designing, leasing, and supporting anti-piracy software to help other software companies protect their intellectual property. It's a business-to-business company, and while he has a virtual assistant helping him, the company is primarily him and his partner, so he has been working a lot of hours. After an initial round of funding, however, they launched last year and are doing well enough that they are considering adding a full-time employee to their team. Andrei has set up a home office and plans to work from home at least three days a week, only going into the office on days when he has meetings, but he can't work and take care of the kids at the same time, so childcare remains an issue.

Maya has a law degree and has passed her state bar, but she hasn't yet practiced law. They put Andrei's career first while she was home with the children, although she kept up with the legal field by doing paralegal work on the side. She's been offered a part-time job with a local law firm that she expects will become full-time within the first year, and she's excited to be getting back into the workforce.

"Right now I'm covering for an attorney who's transitioning into retirement," she told Gunnar. "He's been working part-time himself for this past year, wrapping up projects and, honestly, getting used to the idea of not working all the time anymore. It's too bad he didn't take this cruise," Maya added. "He's someone who never really thought about what he wanted to do when he retired, and I can tell he's already floundering a little. In any case, I've been brought in to pick up the slack, and both the partners and I are using this time to make sure we're a good fit."

"When Maya does start working full-time," Andrei said, "the child-care juggle will become even more difficult to manage. For now, Maya, her mom, and I have pickup, drop-off, and afternoons covered, but there are a lot of moving parts. I'm not sure what we'll do."

"The first thing you're going to do," said Gunnar firmly, "is get life insurance."

"I'm not sure we can afford life insurance," Maya told him.

"You can't afford *not* to have it," he answered. "I know, it feels like you're balancing a house of cards. But this is nothing compared to what it would be if something happened to one of you. You have to protect your children. You need to look at having a minimum of $500K each, and I want you to bump that to $1 million each just as soon as you can. But that $500,000 has got to be the first thing you do when you get home. Neither of you is replaceable, but life insurance can at least keep the devastation of losing someone from becoming a tsunami that destroys your children's future.

"Okay," Gunnar continued, "let's get down to brass tacks. Normally when I do these Reality Checks, I look at the numbers on the table. How much you've already saved, what your assets are, the works."

"It's going to be a short conversation then," Andrei laughed. "We haven't saved much of anything. We're renters and we're both still paying off our student loans."

"But we're poised to be able to start saving," his wife added quickly. "Andrei is finally able to draw a steady salary from his business and I'm going to have a reliable income as well. We borrowed some money from my parents to keep us afloat last year, right before the launch, because we had pretty much wiped out our savings by then. But we'll have finished paying that back by the end of this year. On the plus side, we have learned to live pretty frugally."

"As frugally as you can with two kids," Andrei said.

Gunnar smiled. "I have full faith in you two. For you, the most important investment you can make is in yourselves. To some extent, you've already done that. You sacrificed and pared your budget down so that Andrei could start his business. And it's doing well, right?"

"It's getting there," Andrei acknowledged. "We have a great product and terrific word of mouth."

"Good. You and your partner should be proud of having created something that helps other people. I'm sure you're already thinking about how to grow the company. Part of that growth should be looking at offering a 401(k) plan. You'll be able to participate in that as well, and it's a terrific way to grow your nest egg. I know you have a lot of debt on the table right now, but don't neglect your future. Putting even a little bit aside now, when it has so much time to grow, can make a big difference in thirty years. Let's look at some numbers.

"If you start by investing as little as $200 a month in an index fund, at a 6 percent rate of interest—which is very conservative, well below the stock market's average of 10 percent a year—at the end of thirty years, you'll have invested around $72,000, but you'll have almost $200,000 in savings. Up that even a little, to investing $300 a month, and you'll have almost $300,000 in savings from a $108,000 investment. Investing $500 a month gives you nearly $500,000 in ten years. And remember, I'm using conservative interest rate estimates. Even going up one percentage point, to a 7 percent return each year, adds tens of thousands of dollars to your total savings. Time is your friend, but only if you get started now."

"Once we've finished paying my parents back, we can redirect that monthly payment right into an index fund," Maya said. "We won't even notice it because we've already been setting it aside."

"That's a great idea," said Gunnar. "You want to make saving as effortless as possible."

"Look, that's all true," said Andrei, "but at some point, we're going to want to buy a house. I don't see how we're ever going to get a down payment together if we direct money into retirement. Aren't we always hearing about how important home ownership is?"

"I believe in it," Gunnar told him. "But I also believe you'll be able to do both. What neither of you is taking into account is how to make investing in yourself really pay off. Andrei, we've been talking about your business. What did you learn from launching a successful startup?"

Andrei looked surprised at the question. "Just about everything," he said. "We must've developed twenty different ideas before we landed on this one and knew we had something special. Some of those other ideas were pretty good and some were terrible. Part of the learning curve was figuring out how to tell the difference. For the first year we were putting this together, when our daughter was born, I was working a full-time job with a nonprofit and developing my relationships in the software industry after work and on weekends. So I know how to manage my time pretty well and also how to network. I developed a pitch deck, I created an advisory board, I met with investors . . . it was trial by fire, but in the end, it worked."

"Fantastic!" Gunnar beamed at him. "You now have an expertise other people would kill for. Do you see how you could parlay some of those experiences into articles for professional magazines, keynote lectures, online webinars, a book? You have a lot of charisma and even more energy—this is a great way to channel it, to become known as an expert in your field. This is about more than just the income that lectures and a book could generate, although, particularly in the business world, the teaching circuit can be very lucrative. But every time you go out there and share your knowledge, you are also marketing your product and your company, increasing its potential value."

For the first time on the cruise, Andrei was paying complete atten-tion to what Gunnar was saying. Maya could see her husband working it out; he was coming up with ideas left and right. She smiled as Gunnar turned to her.

"As for you, Maya," he said, "you are well positioned for an impressive career. The key will be to stop seeing yourself as an employee. When you start this job, you will have the choice to see yourself as a part-timer doing the work you're told to do, or to see yourself as someone who brings everything to the table. You've kept up with your field even when you were a full-time mother, and that's amazing. Now you have to double down on that. Be constantly looking to network, make connections that will be important to your firm and to you personally. You want to spend this year making sure this position has real potential and isn't going to be a dead end for you. Set a goal and evaluate every quarter: Are you making connections? Are you learning things that will make you more valuable? Are you the go-to person for some area of expertise? Of course you want to contribute to your employer, but you want to contribute in such a way that your value is both crystal clear and increasing.

"Ultimately, your ability to have all the things you want—being debt-free, owning your own home, being secure in retirement—all of these things will be much easier if you commit to taking ownership of your careers," he told both of them. "I'm not advocating living to work; you have a family, you want to enjoy life. It's not about working harder as much as it is being intentional about how and where you create value, and creating opportunities for that value to be recognized. You can be in a prestigious job that looks great on paper, but there's no room to grow, either professionally or financially. It's just a dead-end job at a higher plateau. Really look for opportunities to shine and keep moving to the next step. You'll do fine."

LECTURE 8: INVESTING IN THE STOCK MARKET

William smiled as he saw the packed auditorium.

"Nice to see so many friendly faces today," he told them. "There's a reason I give this lecture on a day when we don't have a port of call: It wouldn't be fair to the local businesses—you'd all be cutting your visits short. And yet," he added, "learning to invest in the stock market, while important, is not more important than the other advice I've given. But it is more exciting than, say, the Federal Reserve, and I'm glad you're here.

"Let me start by repeating my disclaimer: Nothing I say is meant to be used as specific investment advice. Always do your own due diligence, and that includes when you're working with a broker. If something seems too good to be true, proceed with caution. Bernie Madoff scammed a lot of people—a lot of them friends, people who trusted him on a personal level—with returns that simply couldn't be replicated. Diversifying your investments can't keep you from being taken in by fraud, but it can keep you from losing everything to one bad actor. Also, you'll make mistakes. I've invested in companies I truly believed in and I've been wrong about their prospects. You will be wrong, too. That's okay. To a certain extent, investing in the stock market is not about not making mistakes; it's about getting in the game. It's about ownership.

"This is one of the things that makes the stock market interesting to me. As shareholders, you are part owners—a small part, I'll grant you—in the companies that propel our economy. It's always better to own a piece of the action. That way, when the company grows, so does your stake. When the U.S. economy does well, so do you. You are hitching your star to a massive economic machine, and historically, that has been a path to wealth.

"Also, I gave you an overview of the stock market when I talked about inflation. What that means is that a dollar is worth less and less as time goes on. If you'll recall, the important point—really, the key to everything—is that *very few investments outpace inflation*. Certainly the interest in your savings account won't cut it. And just stuffing bills into your mattress actually means you're losing real value as time goes on. But the stock market traditionally has done *better* than inflation. So taking those bills and putting them to work for you by investing in companies you believe in can help you increase the value of your savings, even taking inflation into account.

"So, yes, I believe that investing in the stock market is something you should seriously consider. I'm sure some of you already own stock. For the others, before you plunk down your first penny—and even if you're already a stockholder—I want you to think about your investment objectives. For one thing, you need to have reasonable expectations. The stock market is a terrible short-term investment—it's akin to gambling, and we all know how I feel about that. But long term, that's different. Long term, the stock market has averaged over

10 percent a year since its inception. Yes, there have been down years, but it always bounces back higher. Compare that 10 percent to whatever interest you're getting at the bank the next time you see your savings account statement. It's a big difference. So first, your expectations have to be that, no, this is not how you're going to quit your job next year. But, yes, consistent investing in the stock market is one way to make sure that in twenty years, you have enough savings to safely retire.

"So, keep your expectations long term, that's number one.

"Number two, decide how much risk you can handle. The conventional wisdom is that the younger you are, the more time there is to make up for losses, so the more risk you can take. What do I mean by 'risk'? Well, for instance, investing in a newer company or in newer technology—things that don't already have a long track record. Those are considered risky because while management has high hopes, they don't have proof that their plans will work. But because of that, early investors may be able to buy the stock low and be rewarded later when the company succeeds. *If* the company succeeds. If it doesn't, you lose your investment. Greater risk and greater potential reward often go hand in hand.

"When you still have a lot of working years ahead of you, the investment loss may not mean so much. Remember, stock investments should never be made with money you need now, or soon, to feed your family or keep a roof over your head. You invest money that you can afford to lose, and to some extent, you hope for the best.

"I'm not going to sugarcoat this: You will lose money, and sometimes you will lose a lot of money. How well prepared you are to survive that loss unscathed is what I consider the determining factor of how much risk you can tolerate. People talk about being able to take risks in the market as if that were a sign of strength, but it's not strength to bet your family's home so you can play with the newest, shiniest stock toy.

"Sit down, do your budget, figure out how much you can invest immediately to get in the game, and then budget a regular amount every month to add to that investment. If you want to take on a weekend job or a side gig to have more money to invest, I won't talk you out of it. But don't stick your hand in the mortgage cookie jar just because someone has an interesting IPO coming up. Being forced to sell stock at a low because you are desperate for the money can wipe out any gains you may have made. And it's demoralizing. Don't put yourself in that position."

William stopped to take a sip of water. He realized his audience was growing restless.

"I know," he told them. "You did not sign up for this cruise so I could tell you not to invest in the stock market. I'm just saying, don't invest money you don't have. Think of your income in jars. You have the jar to spend on food, to spend on rent or a mortgage, to spend on life insurance, utilities, the essentials to keep you safe and warm. And then you have nonessentials: entertainment, new clothes, eating out. Look, if you want to take from that nonessentials jar to invest in the market, I will cheer you on. But it means being intentional; it means actually making a plan to eat out less, to stay home and watch TV or listen to music or invite friends over for a potluck. Or it means making more money or earmarking your next raise or bonus for investment rather than to upgrade the life you're leading. I want you to get in the game, but I want you to be realistic and to understand there will be trade-offs.

"Okay, so you've got some discretionary funds that you can use to get started in the stock market. I mentioned dollar cost averaging earlier—just to refresh your memory, this is when you automatically invest a certain amount every month into a stock or a fund. It takes timing the market out of the equation: High, low, you are always buying a little bit every month. You realize this is money you are investing for the long term; it's not something you'll need for property taxes or even an unexpected emergency—you've been listening to Gunnar, so you have emergency funds set aside for that. Great! So what's next?

"You need to create a framework for a well-diversified asset mix. Which is fancy talk for not putting all your eggs in one basket. Also, you want to create some guidelines for yourself. Are there arenas you want to invest in? Are there sectors you don't? What is an acceptable return on your investment? Are you going to need to spend dividends as you go to supplement your retirement income or will you be reinvesting them? Again, the earlier you start and the less you need any kind of immediate return, the better: You can reinvest your dividends and use them to buy more stock that will, in turn, both appreciate and provide even more dividends down the line. Win-win. But only you know where you are in your financial life.

"So what's a reasonable asset allocation? First of all, you want to keep some of your investment in cash. I know, that doesn't seem to make sense—I just told you how much more return on investment you can historically get in the stock market versus your savings account. But nothing is more flexible than cash, and you want that. You want to be able to have the funds available to buy a stock that you believe is poised to go up, for instance.

"You also want to keep a percentage of your assets invested in fixed income, which means things like government or corporate bonds; certificates of deposit, or CDs; and money market funds. These are generally safe investments but with low yields, sometimes lower than inflation, so be wary. For bonds, the bond is only as good as the entity issuing it. Not all bonds carry the same risks, so do your research before you buy. The lowest-risk bonds also have lower yields, but that's okay. The whole point of bonds is to have some money in investments that have a fairly low risk, but that at least provide more interest than stuffing the dollars in your mattress. Check the bond ratings before you buy.

"Finally, you want to balance the remaining percentage of your funds between U.S. equity and international equity. We are increasingly a global economy and you want to be part of that.

"You also want to divide your assets among different sectors. A sector is a group of stocks that are considered to be in similar industries. Dividing investments up by sectors helps you envision diversification. So, we have a Communications sector. We have Consumer Staples, things like food, beverages, and grocery stores; Consumer Discretionary, which is more luxury items as well as businesses like hotels; Energy; Financial; Healthcare; Industrials, which means airplanes, railroads, defense; Materials, like mining stocks, construction goods, and the makers of chemicals; Real Estate; Information Technology; and Utilities. These are all cornerstone industries, and one way to diversify is to invest in most or all of them. This is what people mean when they talk about a 'balanced portfolio.' When one industry goes down, others will stay the same or even rise, keeping your overall portfolio on an even keel.

"There are other ways to think of balancing your portfolio. You can look at allocating assets among stocks of companies based on their market capitalization. 'Value' stocks are those that, for whatever reason, seem to be trading below their actual potential. For instance, if the CEO of a stock is caught in some kind of scandal, it can lower the stock price without actually having a negative impact on how well the company will do in five years. I think of it as a temporary bargain. A 'growth' stock, on the other hand, is one that has potential that hasn't yet translated to its stock price. Neither one is a sure bet, but both have the potential to outperform the market. Not that you need to outperform the market! If you simply do as well as the market, you are still ahead of inflation and a piggy bank. But it can be a lot of fun to have some holdings that you believe in. And you for sure want some 'core' stocks. 'Big and boring,' that's my motto. Core stocks are reliable, they have a track record of growth, and they're not going anywhere. So having a mix of value, growth, and core stocks is yet another way to think about maintaining a balanced portfolio.

"You also want to establish formal criteria for what a stock has to do to remain in your portfolio, and then monitor your investments. For instance, maybe you want companies to have a ten-year history showing a minimum annual growth of at least 6 percent and at least a 3 percent dividend. You may want to establish a 'watch' list to help you identify potential future purchases. As you go along, evaluate and compare performance results achieved by each of your investments on a regular basis.

"One way to evaluate stock is to look at the price-to-earnings ratio, or P/E. It's what the market is willing to pay—'price'—over the earnings per share of the company. A high price-to-earnings ratio might mean that investors are confident that a stock is going to have high future earnings, or it could mean the stock is overpriced. A low P/E could mean that the stock may be undervalued. You have to compare a stock's P/E to other stocks in the same industry. The average P/E for the S&P 500 has typically been somewhere between thirteen and fifteen, but it varies quite a bit by industry. The nice thing about the P/E ratio is that it's a simple way to get a snapshot of a stock. It's not the only metric you should use. You should always read the prospectus, and if you're serious about investing in the stock market, I recommend reading widely and considering working with a broker who might be able to provide expertise and guidance. But the P/E is a way for you to start getting involved in evaluating stocks, and that's a good muscle to flex.

"I want you to understand the fundamentals. With all the hype about the market and particular stocks or industries, there really is a set of fundamental information that we need to pay attention to:

1. Is the assets-to-debt ratio a burden?

2. Is there available cash to grow the company?

3. What is the return on investment?

4. Are sales and income going up or going down? Obviously, you want the company's income to be increasing.

5. Is the company positioned to stay competitive? Is it advancing in its industry?

6. What is the dividend history?

"You always want to measure the company against similar businesses. Different sectors have different challenges. The computer industry is advancing with new products that require development, while oil companies require leases for proven wells, and so forth. You are not just measuring the company you're interested in—you must measure companies in the same business.

"This is a lot of work, and it's one of the reasons why people rely on brokers. If you do decide on a broker, you need to find one who has the same investing philosophy as you do.

"Another option is to buy mutual funds. A mutual fund may be managed, with managers continually re-evaluating stocks, or it could be an index fund, which simply maintains stocks that mirror a specific index, like the S&P 500 or the Russell 3000, which is the benchmark for basically the entire U.S. stock market. Always make sure you understand the investment, but mutual funds and ETFs, or exchange-traded funds, which also include a variety of companies, can be a way of outsourcing the decision-making in terms of which individual stocks to buy.

"I'm sure you've all heard of the sterling financial advice to 'buy low and sell high.' That's fine and dandy, but it only works if you happen to have a crystal ball to tell you when a stock is going to be low and when it's going to be high. Stocks get hot and cold, they get overbought, they get bashed by natural disasters, they gain or lose a great management team, there are class action suits and product failures; some stocks fall apart while others rebound unexpectedly. It is much, much safer to really look into a stock before you buy it and then hold it for the long term.

"Unlike a crystal ball, self-control is in your power and it can make an incredible difference. If you're really into this, go read Nobel Prize winner Richard Thaler. He makes economics accessible and his contributions to behavioral economics help us understand why we do what we do, even if on the surface it doesn't make rational sense. Good stuff."

William took a moment while his audience caught up with their note-taking. Shirley saw that Betty was taking detailed notes on her laptop, while Lamont took his by hand in a dot grid notebook, illustrating key points with funny drawings and cartoon captions.

"I'm glad we get to share their notes," Shirley whispered to Sam. "There's so much to take in, I can barely keep up!"

"I haven't talked much about bonds today, and I won't," William continued. "Having some bonds in your portfolio makes sense only in that they're a fairly secure way of making a little more interest than with most savings accounts. Again, you want to have them if the stock market tanks and you need the cash—they are a hedge against having to sell at the bottom of the market. But bonds are not an investment that pays big dividends or even, as a rule, keeps pace with inflation. And junk bonds are just that: junk. The companies issuing them have little financial strength, and if they go bankrupt, you lose your investment. Don't buy things just because they're cheap. Figure out why they're cheap first. Is the stock undervalued? Do you believe, based on solid reasoning and some evidence, that it will go up? Great. Is it a junk bond based on promises with no foundation? That's not a good risk to take.

"And while I'm warning you about junk, let me throw in one red flag you will never regret heeding: the hard sell. There are times when someone—maybe someone who makes their living pretending to have a crystal ball for the stock market, or sometimes even a broker you trust—tries to exert pressure to get you to invest in a particular stock for personal or professional reasons that don't have a lot in common with your best interests. Some may even want to do what's called 'churning' your account in order to charge you more fees. They do this by overtrading, or getting you to continually rotate the stocks in your investment account. There is also such a thing as 'reverse churning,' where brokers do as little as possible because they're on a flat fee, and they just want their percentage of assets at the end of the year without actually providing the guidance you're paying them for.

"If your broker makes commissions on transactions, however, that's when churning becomes a potential problem. Be wary when brokers start giving you multiple 'buy alerts,' or telling you to buy because 'there's a lot of activity.' That's not a reason; that's an excuse to get you to move your money around. I see clickbait headlines like 'See How I Beat the Market!' and 'My Secret Weapon for Picking Stocks,' and I just get so frustrated with these people. They imply they have a secret way to read the future, and they pull people in with stock picks that are no more reliable than reading your palm. And any pressure for immediate decisions or warning you that you'll miss out on 'the action'—I mean, if it sounds like a horse race, it probably is.

"Churning is just plain wrong. It is illegal, it is unethical, and I am not going to tell you that you'll never encounter it. It's also very hard to prove. So how do you combat it?

"First, you need to be an active participant in your account. Some people are tempted to give their broker discretionary authority over their accounts, allowing them to trade at will. Don't do that. Make them get your permission to make a change to your account—and if they push back on that, take it as a potential warning sign. Why would they want to make changes to your account without running them by you first? They may have a great answer, there may not be a problem there, but you won't know unless you ask.

"If you don't have the time or the inclination to actively participate, set up an account with an online or discount broker who charges a flat, per-transaction fee and provides no management or guidance. Invest in index funds or the equivalent in a few different sectors, do your dollar cost averaging, and check the fund's performance a couple of times a year. Done. I don't need you to become an expert in investing if that prevents you from even getting in the game. You may find yourself becoming more involved as the years go by, or you may not. What's important is that you find a way to start now.

"In a way, the stock market is your partner. You are providing funds that are necessary for companies and our economy to thrive. In return, the market is providing you with dividends on your investment and an appreciation of your asset. As companies do well, you do well; just remember that the reverse is also true. In any kind of partnership, there may be ups and downs. Don't blame the market for going down. Instead, look at the down times as an opportunity to buy some shares on your watch list that may now be undervalued. Remember that the market going down in the short term doesn't impact your success when what you're playing is the long game.

"Okay, a few quick thoughts to end on, and I will let you go. First, if you have an investment that is underperforming in its sector and the market, don't just sit on it. Evaluate, see if it has the potential to turn around. If it remains something you believe is undervalued and poised to break out, factor that into your decision. If it simply is a laggard, sell it and move on. You don't get brownie points for loyalty.

"Second, bargains are bargains for a reason. Avoid junk bonds and cheap stocks.

"Third, know when you're being sold to. A hard sell is overcompensating for something. Maybe it's a broker who wants to earn more commission by churning, maybe it's a stock that is hiding a poor foundation underneath a glitzy tagline. It helps to strip away to the fundamentals and let the numbers speak for themselves.

"Fourth, diversify. I don't care what else you leave with today—leave with the idea that you need to invest in multiple sectors and in companies both domestic and international. Give up the idea that you are going to pick one perfect stock, invest all your marbles in it, and see it shoot up and make your fortune. It is infinitely more likely that any stock you pick will go up and down and eventually up again. Spreading the risk around different sectors makes eventual success more likely.

"Finally, timing is everything. I don't mean timing the market. Just like picking the one perfect stock, timing the market is a poor substitute for diversification. No, what I mean is using time to your advantage. Be patient. Think long range. There will be highs and lows, and you need to roll with them. Stay the course. The stock market is one place where the optimist has a greater chance of success than the pessimist, because when things get bad, the pessimist will sell at the market low and the optimist will hold through the down times. I'm not saying hang onto an individual stock if it's tanking, but I am saying that, historically, when the entire market has tanked, it has eventually rebounded to ever-increasing heights. If you have a diverse portfolio and a long time frame, you are in a good spot to weather the ups and downs of the market."

AN ABUNDANCE OF OPTIONS

After the stock market lecture, the women met up as planned in the spa. They changed into their robes, then sat together in the spa lounge and looked over the menu of options.

"There's so much to choose from!" Maya exclaimed. "Massages, hot stones, facials, a steam room, a Jacuzzi and a sauna—I don't even know where to start."

"That's how I felt leaving William's lecture today," Shirley admitted. "There are so many stocks in so many—what did he call them, sectors? I'm just not sure where to begin."

"Well, I don't know if I'm someone you should take financial advice from," laughed Betty. "I'm just as new to this game as you are. But Joe and I have decided that we're going to start with an index fund. That seems to me to be a good way to get instant diversification. And then we're going to set up a watch list of individual stocks and start buying the ones we like a little at a time. Besides," she added, "it will give us a new hobby. We're not going to be traveling the world on what we've managed to save for retirement."

"Do you want to travel the world?" Rose asked.

"No . . ." Betty responded thoughtfully. "I never really put things off in my head, like, 'Oh, I'll wait to do that fun thing until we've retired.' Joe and I have traveled a bit, and we took this cruise, for instance, and it's been great. We both enjoy working on the house as well, and if we had a bit more money, I would love a remodeled kitchen. But mostly, I want to live near my family, maybe have a little more time for reading, which I don't get to do much during the school year. And not have to worry that we'll outlive our savings. To me, that's the real concern."

"I'm excited to look at the stock market," Gabriela said. "Lamont and I have been talking about diving in for a long time now, but we didn't know where to begin. Breaking it down into sectors and making sure we have something in each bucket, if you will—it feels right. I'm someone who has a Plan A, a Plan B, and if they don't work, Plans C through Z. Looking at diversification that way, and that it's how you protect yourself when things go haywire in one industry or even the market as a whole, makes a lot of sense to me."

"But how will you know which stocks to pick?" asked Maya.

Gabriela shrugged. "We're going to start by listing all the companies we believe in, some because we use them a lot, some because we think the world is moving in that direction. Like Betty and Joe, we'll put together a watch list, but we're also going to start right away when we get back. We've decided to open up an account with an online broker and have a set amount deposited from our checking account each month. That way, we have a cash reserve and a monthly reminder to check over our brokerage account and re-evaluate. There are a couple of stocks we know we want—one tech, one healthcare—so we're going to get those first, and then slowly buy in other sectors. We figure by this time next year, we'll have some holdings across the board and then we can start refining. I am loving this—this is the push we needed to really get serious about making our money work for us."

Shirley nodded. "Not just making our money work," she said, "but other assets as well. Sam and I have a duplex from when we first were married. We hung onto it and rented it out, but we never really thought much about it or did anything with it, other than cash the rent and pay the property bills, and occasionally fixed a screen door. We even let Sam's brother live there rent-free for a couple of months when he was going through a personal crisis. That actually cost us money! After talking to Gunnar, we realized that real estate is an asset that could do a lot more for us. We just have to be willing to put in the effort."

Rose sighed. "I think the most interesting thing about this cruise is how there is something for each of us to learn. I'm completely uninterested in the stock market, but this cruise has still given me a lot to think about. Peter and I have been talking about taking a family trip for years, but we always put it off until a 'better' time. After we worked with Gunnar on our Reality Check, we realized there is no better time than right now. To me, that has been such a gift—taking the uncertainty and dithering away from it. It's something we want to do, and financially we can pull it off. And frankly I don't know how much time I may have left. I don't want to call the trip a 'bucket list' item, but I have realized that for me, it's not about making sure Peter and our son and grandchildren have enough money, but rather that they have enough happy memories of time we all spent together. That's the legacy I'm thinking about."

The women were quiet for a moment. Gabriela put her hand over Rose's.

"Legacy isn't a bad thing for any of us to think about," Gabriela said quietly. "It gives you a lens that makes decision-making crystal clear."

"Do you know," Betty said, "that gives me an idea. I know a lot of retired teachers, many of whom are just puttering around now that they're out of the classroom. I've always wanted to do something to help some of the kids in our district who aren't doing well but can't afford private tutoring. I wonder if I could start a nonprofit to offer tutoring."

"If anyone could," Rose laughed, "it would be you, Betty! I've never seen anyone as organized in my life."

"Using our skills to make the world better is another benefit of having financial freedom," Maya said thoughtfully. "When you are just focused on survival—and I have to tell you, having two small children and a husband with a startup has been really tough financially—you don't have the time or energy to think about how you can make a difference in other people's lives. My parents have been helping us a little financially and a lot in terms of daily support. I've been able to do paralegal work on the side because my mom comes over and watches the kids a couple of afternoons a week, and Andrei and I clean the house and cook a week's worth of meals on Sundays when my folks have the kids over to their house. We both work every evening once the kids are in bed as well. Not that I'd trade my family for anything, but it's been an exhausting few years. I feel like this cruise came at the perfect time for us, when we are poised to take a breath and can make some decisions beyond just getting through the day."

"This cruise has been eye-opening for so many reasons," Shirley said. "Financial guidance, options we'd never thought about before, giving us new ways of looking at our assets, forcing us to decide on some financial goals. So much to think about, so many choices to make!"

"And one of those choices is which massage I'm going to have today!" Rose laughed. "Hot stone massage, here I come."

Dinner: Viva Italia

Dinner that night was an Italian-themed affair. Chef Luigi outdid himself. There were steamed clams with garlic and herbs, bruschetta with tomato and garlic, individual pepperoni pizzas, cioppino, osso buco, and seafood fettuccine with lobster and asparagus spears.

But the real treat of the evening came as the dessert tray was being rolled out. The dessert table included cannoli, rum cake, and biscotti, as well as freshly brewed coffee. Three men appeared in tuxedos, all looking very dapper, with an air of being from the 1940s or 1950s. They took turns singing songs made famous by Italian American singer Perry Como. One of them did a wonderful impersonation of Como, not just vocally, but in his mannerisms as well. The singing was excellent, and some of the older passengers felt nostalgic hearing renditions of their favorite songs, like "When You Were Sweet Sixteen," "And I Love You So," and "Some Enchanted Evening." Peter and Rose, in particular, were absolutely delighted with the show.

Chef Luigi visited their table with coffee refills after the singing was over. "This is my favorite dinner to serve," he said, "and my favorite night on the cruise. I get to share some of the wonders of Italy with you. My father was born there, and I still have family, and I'll tell you something else—I have been listening to William's advice on these cruises and I am on track to be able to retire someday in Italy. Now that will be a dream come true!"

He left them, moving on to other guests, but the chef had sparked a discussion about Italy.

"Italy is one of the great postwar success stories," Peter said thoughtfully. "Their economy was in shambles after World War II."

"They didn't have anywhere to go but up," said Joe. "Much like me and Betty now."

Betty rolled her eyes. "We're not in that bad shape," she told him. "But if you want to follow Italy's example, that's fine by me. They made the most of what they had, and we can do that, too."

"I don't know much about it," said Andrei. "How did they get their economy back on its feet?"

"Well, the United States helped," Sam said. "Food and direct aid from the U.S. helped to rebuild the steel industry and other basics the Italian economy needed to thrive."

"They also started educating women," explained Betty. "Most girls didn't start going to secondary schools until the 1960s, and lots of studies have found that educating girls leads to better economic outcomes for emerging countries—and that's what Italy was at the time. Every dollar invested in a girl's secondary education ends up increasing a country's gross domestic product by almost three dollars. That's some bang for your buck."

"And it's all because of education, which is where you shine," Rose told her.

"That's true," agreed Betty. "But it's also about making use of your resources. Leaving girls without education leaves so much potential behind."

"Italy used its other resources as well, including its heritage," added Sam. "Once the currency stabilized after the war, they started bringing in tourists. Tourism accounts for around 10 to 12 percent of Italy's GDP every year."

"They also produced beautiful things," said Maya. "Italian couture is the height of fashion and shoes."

"Don't forget cars!" added Lamont. "Maserati, Lamborghini—those are tops."

"That's right," agreed Peter. "They developed quality products and branded them as exclusive. They also invested in infrastructure, especially in the south. They built roads that connected different areas of the country and created a sense of unity and purpose. Everyone was moving forward together."

"And they took care of their families," added Rose.

"It seems to me," Lamont said, "that the same things that led to Italy's success would lead to individual success: Make the most of your resources, educate yourself, create quality, develop a reputation for excellence, take care of your family, and work to connect people so we can all move forward together."

"Great metaphor," said Joe.

"Italy really is a lovely country," added Rose. "Maybe that's where we should take the family?" she asked her husband.

Peter nodded. "It would certainly be the trip of a lifetime."

CHAPTER NINE

WHAT IS "NORMAL"?

The Morning Ritual

The men met up for their usual tour around the top deck, but none of them seemed enthusiastic that day. They realized that the cruise would soon be over, and while they were sorry to see it end, they also were already thinking about what they'd do when they got home.

"This is a terrible way for us to 'enjoy the journey,'" Lamont commented. "Rachael would not be happy with us. Here we are, on the deck of this beautiful ship, enjoying the early morning sunshine, and what are we thinking about? Going home."

"Not just going home," Sam said. "I'm actually thinking about how I have to fix the bathroom door so that it closes properly. Especially if we're going to rent out a room, we don't want doors that stick."

"Guilty as charged, Lamont," Peter laughed. "I was thinking about putting in a security system. I need to call some friends to see which company they use. I'm already annoyed at the time it'll take me, and I'm still on vacation!"

"I've got yardwork on my plate," Joe said. "I'm excited about it—some of the gardens we've seen have been amazing—but yes, it's also work I've been putting off. What about you, Andrei?"

"I'm thinking about making my will," he answered.

The other men stopped to look at him.

"Way to up the stakes," Lamont said. "You win."

Andrei shrugged. "I've spent so much of the last couple of years thinking about building the foundation to my business . . . I've taken the foundation of my family a little bit for granted. Soon as we get home, I need to make sure they're taken care of no matter what—life insurance, wills. I should probably see if I need insurance in my business, too, in case something happens to me. Not things we want to think of, but the last thing I'd want would be for Maya to have to deal with a financial catastrophe on top of losing me. This is a gift I can give her—one I hope she'll never need!"

Ice Show

The river had been too high the night before for the ship to set out in time to make their port of call that day, so to make up for missing the shore excursions, Chef Luigi and one of his sous-chefs put on an exhibition in the dining room. First, they set several blocks of ice on the table. The sous-chef started chiseling the ice while Luigi set up an ice bar with vodka bottles on a counter made from a slab of ice. The group helped themselves to shots of cold vodka while the sous-chef worked.

"No vodka for him," joked Luigi. "Who knows what he'd chisel? We want a work of art here, not a pile of ice cubes."

Meanwhile, Luigi's assistant had brought out a tray of vegetables. Luigi gave a demonstration on how to carve a floral bouquet out of carrots, radishes, cucumbers, and other vegetables.

"Wow," said Gabriela. "It really is amazing. You can make anything beautiful with a little bit of work."

"Another metaphor?" asked her husband.

"I don't know if they meant it to be or if we're just prepped to see metaphors everywhere after this last week," Gabriela answered. "But it is getting me thinking. You know how we'd been talking about redoing the living room?"

Lamont nodded. "You've been collecting ideas for months now."

"What if we did it without spending any money?"

"You want to ask Luigi to come carve up the furniture?" Lamont joked.

Gabriela rolled her eyes at him. "You're an artist," she said. "You have a great eye for color and form, and because of that, we have some really nice stuff. I think we should make the most of what we have, make it special, rather than tossing things or putting them in storage and starting over. Maybe invest in a new coat of paint—"

"A bright color," Lamont cut in. "Something that pops."

"Exactly!" agreed Gabriela. "And rearrange the furniture to reflect how we really use the space instead of how we think it should look."

"Like all those pictures you've spent months gathering?" teased Lamont.

"Maybe they showed me what I didn't want," his wife countered. "I think it's important that we make the most of what we have, but also that we make choices that reflect who we are as individuals and how we use that room. We can take that turnip and transform it into a rose!"

Lamont laughed. They turned to see that the sous-chef had finished, and the ice blocks had been transformed into a Papa Bear, a Mama Bear, a Baby Bear, and an upside-down bowl of porridge.

"I guess that's our sign, Goldilocks," Lamont said. "It's not about what we think is 'normal.' It's about deciding intentionally on what we like and making sure the fit is just right."

MAPPING IT ONTO YOUR OWN LIFE

Gunnar and Rachael held an informal salon in the lounge that afternoon.

"It's a free-for-all," Gunnar said cheerfully as the passengers walked in. "A chance for you to ask your questions and for us to have a chance to impart any wisdom that didn't seem to fit into any of our other talks. Grab a drink and take a chair."

They did. Some of them were already thinking of questions to ask. Maya was the first to raise her hand.

"What about debt?" she asked. "I realize many of the people on this cruise already have their houses paid off, as well as their student loans, but Andrei and I are not in that camp. Can you talk about how we can find the money to invest when we still need to pay off a good chunk of debt?"

"That is a great question," said Rachael, "and one I'm going to throw to Gunnar, because this is right up his alley."

Gunnar laughed. "I'd argue with her," he said, "but she's not wrong. I know a lot about debt. I carried a lot of debt for years. And I agree with you—one of the biggest obstacles in a family budget is debt.

"This is probably not the first time you've heard this, but there is good debt and bad debt. Let's start with the worst kind of debt: payday loans. If there is one top reason to create an emergency financial cushion, it's to be able to avoid payday loans. They are predatory lending, which, in a nutshell, means that the interest rates are so high, you will end up paying back three to six times more than the amount you borrowed. Look, if you need to borrow $100 to pay a bill, where are you going to find $300 or $400 to pay back that loan? Stay away from predatory lenders, that's rule number one.

"Rule number two, cut up your credit cards. If you're not going to pay them off in full every month, the interest rate on cards is, yes, less than a predatory loan, but it still becomes harder and harder to stay ahead of the game. You can find yourself in a lot of debt very quickly from running up your cards.

"If you don't want to cut them up, stick them in an envelope, seal it, and put it somewhere that's difficult to access. You want to buy yourself time to rethink the purchase before you pull out the card. Write on the envelope something like, 'Are you sure you want to still be paying for this in a year?' If the answer's no—and it should always be no!—put the card away. Again, an emergency savings fund will help keep you from having to rely on credit or predatory loans that will just end up making your life more difficult. It's wrong that companies prey on those who can least afford it, but it is up to you to protect yourself. Do whatever it takes to build up a financial cushion. You won't regret it.

"Rule number three, pay down your debt when you can, based on the interest rate. If you have a car loan with a zero percent interest rate, sure, it remains a drag on your budget, but it's not getting worse with time. In fact, you're probably paying for it with increasingly cheaper dollars as inflation creeps in. If you have the extra money to pay it off early, maybe that money could be better invested in something that will earn you interest or dividends. Look at all your options.

"Student loan debt, on the other hand, is above inflation and current interest rates, so it's in your best interest to pay it down. Most student loans are federal loans, so I'll just talk about them: The rates peaked in the 1980s at 14 percent, which is more than twice as high as it is now. If you have any loans that are higher than the current rate, it's worth looking into refinancing them; by the latest statistic I saw, more than half of all borrowers are eligible for refinancing, and it can save you a lot down the line. If you can't or don't want to refinance, pay it off early. All education loans in this country, both federal and private, allow you to pay them down—that means paying extra every month—or pay them off without having to pay a prepayment penalty fee. Take advantage. Yes, it may mean money is tight in the short term, but not lugging that debt along with you will free up so many options in the long term."

Rachael took the opportunity to add to the conversation. "The only thing not to do, never to do," she said, "is sacrifice your emergency fund to pay down debt. Emergency savings give you options when you otherwise have very few. Guard that with your life."

"Great point," Gunnar agreed. "Finally, let me talk about what is likely to be your biggest debt: your mortgage on your home. Most of you have already purchased a home, but for those who haven't yet, let me mention something we don't talk about enough: property taxes. When you are figuring out how much you can afford to pay toward your mortgage every month, you need to add in extra money that you should set aside every month to cover annual property tax bills. Look, it's not that I don't want you to own a house, I really do; it has histori-cally been an excellent investment and, again, it's something that gives you options over time. But I don't want you to buy a house you think you can afford only to find yourself scrambling because you didn't factor in taxes. Divide the annual property tax by twelve and set that much aside every month in an account you won't—or can't—touch until it's time to pay your property tax.

"Back to the mortgage itself. Mortgage rates go up and down; if you're lucky enough to lock in a low rate, do it. If not, like with student debt, it's worth looking into refinancing when interest rates tumble. But no matter what your loan's rate is, one thing you have control over is how soon you pay it off. An extra thousand a month doesn't just cut the length of time you're paying the mortgage—it also cuts the amount of interest you pay by a substantial amount.

"For instance, even at a low interest rate of 3.27 percent, if your mortgage balance is $240,000, paying it off in twenty years means you'll pay a total of $327,289, balance plus interest. If you pay roughly an extra thousand a month, you'll pay it off in just ten years and the total amount you've paid is now $281,699, balance plus interest. That's a savings of $45,590. For some people, that's an entire year's salary. And the higher your balance, the bigger the difference."

"That's true," said Shirley, "but it's also a big ask. An extra thousand or more a month? We would never have been able to afford that when we first got our house."

Gunnar smiled. "I'm not going to argue with that. It's very tough to carve out the kind of money that will save you money; that's why predatory loans like payday advances still exist. But that doesn't mean you shouldn't understand the trade-offs. Look, when it comes to something like building your emergency savings, I am all about doing whatever it takes. In fact, let me turn the spotlight over to Rachael to talk about that."

Rachael nodded and looked out at her audience. "Shirley, I agree with you and Gunnar. Yes, it is a big ask. But let me start with a smaller ask, and that is: Ask yourself what can you do to bring in an extra hundred dollars a month. That's twenty-five dollars a week. Can you do that? Chances are, the answer is yes.

"Asking yourself questions that seem reasonable gets your head in a space to come up with answers. What are some things you could do to make an extra twenty-five dollars every week? If you have small children, could you watch another child a few hours a week? If you have a dog, can you walk someone else's dog at the same time? Can you tutor in a subject you know well? Teach an extra yoga class on Zoom? Start by looking at all the things you already do professionally and personally, and see if there isn't a way to slip one more paying customer into the mix.

"Once you do that, chances are you'll actually be making more than an extra twenty-five dollars every week. Success! Now it's just about refining it. Is there an even easier way to make maybe a little more money? Maybe look to your talents and your passions. Is there a way to sell your embroidery on Etsy? To write a web comic or a niche newsletter with a paywall for people to subscribe to your work? To take what you do at work and open up a side business doing it freelance for other people? For instance, if you're a CPA, chances are your friends and family want you to do their taxes for them. There is no shame in charging for that! They should at least pay you for your time, which is the most valuable asset you have.

"Women, in particular, are encouraged to give their time away to anyone who asks for it, and I want you to stop that now. You can help someone and still be compensated for your time. You are still a good person. It still counts. In my book, it counts even more if you're taking care of your financial well-being while also taking care of others.

"The most important thing is that you treat whatever extra money you bring in as untouchable. Open a separate savings account if you can and deposit the extra cash directly into it. Resist the temptation to spend it on anything; that money is spoken for! It is your future. Do this for as long as it takes to build up your emergency savings account. Aim for at least six months of living expenses. Yes, it'll be hard, but you'll start to see the savings grow and you'll know you are protecting yourself from future disasters."

She nodded to Gunnar, and he picked up the thread. "Some people will tell you that you should always have a couple of jobs going, so you can sock away money that you can use to build your financial empire, be it a new business, a real estate investment, or a stock portfolio."

"William will tell you to do that," Rachael added.

Gunnar laughed. "Yes, William would probably tell you to do that. And if you want to, be my guest. There are, I think, times in our lives when we are capable of working crazy hours, two or three jobs, a couple of side hustles. But I think it's a mistake to expect ourselves to do that all the time. There are seasons when we can't—when we have small children or a parent who needs caregiving, for instance. Or when our primary job is intense and demanding, or spills over into our nights and weekends. Personally, I think that doing whatever you can to build your emergency savings isn't just valuable in terms of money. I think it lets you see what options you have beyond your single job. You may be less committed to being an assistant for a demanding or unpredictable boss when you realize you can make almost as much money on the weekends performing at children's birthday parties. That, too, offers you financial freedom: the realization that you have options.

"But ultimately, I don't think trading time for money is the way you'll get rich. It can be the way to give you the financial cushion to protect yourself, and it can provide the foundation for doing something that can transform your life financially. But just working the hamster wheel, even with multiple jobs, is not the thing itself that will pay off in a transformative way.

"What I believe is that you should invest in yourself. You are your greatest asset. Finding a higher-paying job will pay dividends for decades, and how you do that is by spending your free time building your skills and your network. Sometimes a side hustle will help with both of those, but not always. You need to evaluate what you need to move forward in your career, in terms of experience, knowledge, credentials, and mentors. Spending your extra time getting those things taken care of can pay off far more than spending your weekends as a rideshare driver.

"Speaking of driving, I had a friend who was a delivery driver, and let me tell you, he was tired of working for minimum wage and tips. My advice to him was to invest in his own truck. Independent delivery drivers with their own trucks or cargo vans can make a lot more than drivers who drive company trucks, but even more than that, being your own boss changes your perspective and your sense of self-worth. Believe in yourself and treat yourself as a valuable asset. That is a fundamental strategy to increase your net worth."

Joe raised his hand. "That's all well and good for people like Lamont and Maya," he said. "They're at the early stages of their careers. Me, I just retired. I don't want either of us to have to keep working into our eighties just to make sure we don't outlive our savings."

"Joe, that's a great point," Gunnar answered. "I certainly don't want that for any of you. For all the planning we do here to protect your financial future, there is always the possibility that something could go wrong. We've seen it happen. Over the years, negative financial cycles in the economy have created financial disruptions and costly consequences. On a personal level, things happen: disasters, health challenges, life throwing you a curveball. One backup plan I want you all to keep in your back pocket is the idea of a reverse mortgage.

"You own your house, right, Joe? This is one of the reasons why I am a big believer in home ownership. Your house is a tremendous asset. You can rent out a room for someone to live in or you can rent out your living room to groups who need a place to meet—you won't make a lot doing that, but it could be a little extra income. If you're really pressed, maybe you can go live with relatives for a year and rent out your entire house. I know a couple who did that when they found themselves both out of work, and it paid enough to cover the mortgage and property taxes and still have a little to tide them over while they got back on their feet. It wasn't the best year of their lives, but it also wasn't forever. They used what they had to see themselves through.

"So, FYI, if someone tries to convince you that renting a home is just like buying one—I have actually seen people claim that you're only 'renting' your home from the bank when you buy a house—I want you to get very skeptical about what they're pushing. Because when you rent, you do not build equity, and when you buy, you do. Sure, you're paying interest on the loan, but you're also building an asset for your future self. And when the value of your house goes up, unlike if you were renting, your mortgage does *not* go up. On the contrary, it's your equity that goes up, value that you can call upon later. So call that out for the lie it is. Home ownership is a cornerstone financial asset. Renting temporarily keeps a roof over your head.

"Okay, back to reverse mortgages. The official name is a home equity conversion mortgage, or HECM, and it's a government program under the Federal Housing Administration. You have to be over sixty-two years of age and you have to own your home outright or have, at worst, a small mortgage balance, and the house has to be your primary residence. There are a few other requirements, but they have you sit down with an advisor before you get the loan to make sure you understand the ramifications.

"Essentially, an HECM gives you a loan with your house as collateral. Over the years, your mortgage payments haven't just been keeping up with the interest—they've been paying down the principal. Add to that, your home has probably increased in value. So even if you haven't yet paid off your mortgage in full, chances are you have a good amount of equity in your home. This equity can be your safety net if you need it because the amount you can borrow for an HECM depends on two things: the equity in the house and your age. You will get a certain amount of money every month for as long as you live in your home. Best of all, no payments on the reverse mortgage are required until the last eligible person on the loan no longer lives in the home. When you move or both pass away, the house is sold to make good on the loan. There are some expenses involved, including mortgage insurance premiums, but typically they are taken out of the loan.

"For seniors who don't have enough monthly income to get by, this is a fantastic way to be able to stay in your own home while increasing your income so you can meet other obligations. If your circumstances change, you can pay off the loan; if they don't, you or your estate will still get any difference between the loan balance and the sale amount of your house when it's sold. Because you're not repaying the money, there is virtually no chance of being evicted with an HECM, as opposed to a regular mortgage, although you do have to keep up with insurance and property taxes. But you would have to do that anyway. If you're still paying a traditional mortgage, that would be paid off through this loan, freeing up your cash flow. You can choose to take the money in a lump sum, which I don't recommend unless you have an emergency requiring cash, such as falling behind on your property taxes. You can also choose what I recommend, which is taking the money out in monthly allotments. Or you can use it to set up a line of credit.

"One benefit of choosing to take the loan in regular monthly payments is that you won't suddenly have a lump sum that you might be tempted to spend on a splurge for yourself, or more likely—I've seen this happen a lot—for your friends or family. Again, that lump-sum option remains available for an emergency, but I believe the best use is as a little extra money every month to supplement your retirement income and make your golden years easier. And that, my friends, is what I want for all of you."

Reality Check: Gabriela and Lamont

Gabriela and Lamont were Gunnar's last Reality Check of the cruise. He greeted them warmly.

"Thank you for taking the time to work with us," Gabriela said. "We've been so impressed with the advice you've given other people, we're eager to see what you have for us."

"It's a pleasure working with everyone," Gunnar said. "And so interesting to me to get to brainstorm with people at every possible stage of their working lives. You and Lamont are young, so some of the advice I gave to Maya and Andrei will also apply to you."

"I don't have Andrei's charisma," Lamont warned him. "I'm not going to take the lecture circuit by storm."

"Ah, but my advice is always to double down on what you're good at," Gunnar reminded him. "Andrei has a natural ability to talk to people, to be out in front. You're an artist, and there's a whole skill set that comes with that. On this cruise, we talk a lot about assets like houses and stock portfolios, but I believe deeply in our internal assets, too."

> Both Lamont and Gabriela are in their early forties. Gabriela is a small business owner. She runs a boutique temp agency for highly trained CPAs. The agency has three employees in addition to Gabriela and a roster of around thirty temps. Gabriela opened her business six years ago; the first two years, she drew a very nominal salary, but for the last four, she has made $75K per year.

Lamont is a freelance graphic artist. He worked in advertising for a number of years, including the time when Gabriela was getting the temp agency up and running, but he doesn't like office politics and always planned to open his own freelance studio. Over the last four years, since he went solo as an artist and graphic designer, he has had good years and bad ones. One year, he had almost more work than he could handle and brought in $100K before taxes; another year, he only netted $10K. Most years have been somewhere in the middle.

They owe $400K on their house, have just paid off their student debt from graduate school, and have two car payments. They have no children.

"Stability is the great thing we lack," Lamont told Gunnar. "I get so much work that I burn out, and then I get no work and have to hustle, which is also exhausting."

"As for me," Gabriela said, "the business is doing well, but cash flow is always tight. I keep pumping money into the business—I mean, I know it's working because we keep growing, but it feels like a bottomless pit, which is a little scary."

"There are a few things I want both of you to think about," Gunnar said. "The first is building a business plan. Not a pie-in-the-sky thing to show investors—although if you want to, Andrei is the man for pitch decks!—but a plan that centers your business within the actual life you want to lead. I'm guessing there are times when you're both working crazy hours."

"That's most of the time," Gabriela said. "We barely see each other. That was one of the allures of taking this trip."

"Look, that's fine if you're living for work," said Gunnar. "Some people do. But if that's not what you love, if that's not how you want to define your life, that's okay, too. You need to decide how your business fits into your life, and then you need to make a plan to build the life you want around it.

"Let me give you an example: Lamont, the feast-or-famine aspect of your business, do you like that? Does that serve you?"

Lamont answered immediately. "Not at all."

"Okay. Now, I'm just spitballing here," Gunnar said, "but my guess is that when you're working on a project, you spend little to no time prospecting. That is, reaching out to potential clients, maybe doing some interesting personal projects that you share with the larger world, either online or at events, and generally getting yourself out there looking for work."

Lamont looked at him blankly. "Well . . . no," he answered. "Why would I look for work when I have work?"

"Exactly!" Gunnar said. "And then when you don't have work, how often do you say no to a project?"

"Never."

"Right. And that is the problem—not just for you, for a lot of people, whether they're working on their own or for someone else. When you have a job, you don't bother doing the foundational things to build your network and make yourself visible, to let the world know what your special skills are, because, as you said, why look for work when the work is already here? But that way of life, of working for only one employer for your whole career, that is no longer the way the system works.

"I've heard it said that you need to start building your network six months before you actually need it. I would go so far as to say that building your network is something you need to bake into your everyday life, because you will never *not* need it. Sometimes you'll reach out looking for a new restaurant to try or recommendations for a dentist or even a financial cruise. Other times, you'll need it to help find clients or a new job. Building your network is like building your savings—slow and steady gets there in the end."

"So what you're saying," Lamont said, "is that if I put together a plan that includes prospecting and working on my own projects, it will even out the extremes of too much work versus no work at all?"

"Well, actually," Gunnar admitted, "it'll probably lead to more work rather than less, but that's where the second half of your new plan comes in. You need to learn to say no to people."

"I've been telling him that for two years," Gabriela laughed.

"It's hard to say no to clients," Lamont protested. "I don't like to turn down work."

"Right, I get it, and that is a decent strategy when you're building a business," Gunnar agreed. "But at some point, you have to start getting a little pickier about your clients. The first to go are ones who don't pay on time. Any client who hassles you about your fee, you need to be too busy for. Normally, I would suggest developing a referral program with colleagues who also do great work, so that you're not leaving a former client in the lurch—you are instead sending them over to someone else who can meet their needs. But for clients who think it's okay to stiff you or make you wait well beyond the terms of your agreement, you can instead let them know: new policy, your rates have gone up, and by the way, you need to be paid 50 percent upfront. Most will self-select out of that pool. And if they don't, excellent—your rate just went up.

"After that, think about the work that doesn't really play to your strengths. Could you hire someone who is good at that to take on those projects? I want you to think of ways to expand your business without running yourself into the ground. You also want to focus on what you do best. What do you bring to the table that is unique and special? Double down on that, because your genius is what sets you apart and what will command bigger fees and create a larger platform for you down the line."

Gunnar turned to Gabriela. "For you, I know the last several years have been about getting your business up and running, but now is the perfect time to start thinking even bigger. Let me give you an example.

"A middle-aged couple came to me wanting to earn more money. As it was, they had a successful delicatessen. The husband had recently had a health scare and feared he wasn't leaving enough for his family. The way I saw it, the couple had three great possibilities.

"First, they could set up a franchise using the formula they had successfully developed—menu, size, recipes, research into locations— to open up more delis. Second, they could cook up some of their recipes and start selling their products online or to other delis. Third, they could add lines of retail items like cookware or novelties to sell at their store. Ideally, they would explore some combination of all three.

"Now, in your line of business, selling novelties is out, but the other two still hold. You could franchise, opening up other temp agencies along the lines of what you're doing now: small, highly trained, top-quality service to the clients you work with. I would suggest niching down even further to make it easier to differentiate yourself and also find your ideal customers—which are businesses needing accounting temps.

"In addition to franchising, you can bottle, if you will, what you do best. I noticed that you offer ongoing education to your temps. Can you teach classes virtually and sell those modules to other temp agencies in noncompeting markets? Can you write a book? Can you start a social group of entrepreneurial women to meet once a month to swap war stories and best practices? How can you position yourself as well as your company in the top echelons of your field?

"This is what I mean by making a plan that incorporates your business into your life. Who do you want to be in this world? How can the work you do support that, both professionally and financially?

"The last thing I want you to do is find some mentors. People tend to hang out with people their own age, and because younger people aren't talking to older, wiser people, they're often doomed to repeat the mistakes made by those who came before them. So talk to older people. Find some folks who are in your professional orbit who are older than you, ideally people who are retired or on the verge of retirement. Most would probably love to share their wisdom with you!

"I want both of you to find at least three people who are a little, or a lot, further down the road than you are professionally and in terms of life lived. Take them to lunch. Ask them questions. Listen to their advice. They can save you a lot of time down the line."

LECTURE 9: WHAT IS "NORMAL"?

Everyone gathered in the auditorium that evening to listen to the final lecture. William smiled as he looked at their faces for the last time.

"I hope you've enjoyed this cruise," he said. The applause was immediate. "Well, that probably has a lot more to do with Chef Luigi and Captain Olson than with me, but I'll take applause wherever I can get it. Today, I want to wrap up some ideas about the economy and leave you with some final pieces of advice.

"I hope by now you have a better sense of how the economy is working beneath the surface. We can't avoid down times, either in life or in the economy, but we can make better decisions if we know our options. And there are always options. The earlier you start taking action, the more options you have, but there is always something you can do to improve whatever financial situation you find yourself going through.

"First, I want you to understand that everything is interconnected. For instance, we were talking about inflation, right? Well, one possibility is what's called an inflationary spiral, where workers demand higher wages, and when they get better wages, they find they have more disposable income, so they want to buy stuff. As the demand for stuff—and that could be anything from diamonds, gold, or silver to smartphones to real estate—as the demand increases, the prices go up. Which, of course, leads to people no longer being able to afford these things, and a demand renews for higher wages. Now, if you're a buyer, you are not happy that everything costs more. But on the other hand, you're paying your mortgage with cheaper dollars.

"Low demand, on the other hand, can mean there's a surplus of goods and suddenly prices begin to sink. A deflationary spiral can lead to a recession, but at the same time, businesses may be able to hire cheaper labor, and depressed property values can be a real opportunity for buyers. The economy is never perfectly balanced and you have to look for ways to thrive no matter what it's doing.

"I do have a vision for what would be a perfect economy, because of course I do. This is my passion, and I cannot believe I haven't started a book club yet with all the great economists. Richard Thaler! John Maynard Keynes! Elinor Ostrom! I could talk about this stuff all day—as I'm sure you've gathered by now.

"My perspective of a healthy economy would be to use regulation and the influence it can provide to limit the swings, the highs and lows that disrupt the economy. Normal would be an unemployment rate around 3 percent, which allows for some employment turnover but means most people are stable in their positions. I like interest rates around 5 percent for investment, because it induces people to save. Historically low interest rates may be great for mortgages, but not everyone has a mortgage, whereas everyone needs to save more. If I could wave a magic wand, I would keep inflation between 1 percent and 2 percent to ease the burden of debt, and I'd make sure the gross domestic product hovered at 2 percent, showing a growing economy. Finally, I think a price/earnings ratio of 10 percent establishes a fair return on investment.

"Ultimately, I believe in the concept of a non-zero-sum game. Now, a zero-sum game, you've probably heard of. Winner takes all, loser goes home. The whole idea of 'somebody is a winner only if someone else is a loser,' that's a zero-sum game.

"But I invite you to think instead of the economy, of your business, and of life as being a non-zero-sum game. That's a game where the outcome is good for everyone. I don't believe you can have a healthy economy constantly pitting management against labor, or buyer against seller. Take the stock market, for instance. You invest your money in a company by buying stock. They use your money to build the company so that your stock is worth more. That's a non-zero-sum outcome, whereby both of you benefit.

"The same can be true in workplace negotiations. I know that historically, unions and management have been understood to be in opposition, but I don't believe that has to be the case. I believe sitting down at the table together and really listening to each other can lead to outcomes that are win-win. Because it doesn't help the workers if production slows because the company can't meet union demands, and it doesn't help the company if there are injuries or high turnover rates on the job because of unacceptable working conditions. The more we look for ways to create win-win moments in our own lives, the better off we'll all be. Truly, a win-win for the economy and the nation.

"Another thing I want you to do is calm down about investing. There is so much fear and uncertainty around the stock market. People either get too invested in it, seeing it as a get-rich-quick scheme—which it most definitely is not—or they tend to avoid it altogether. You have to be in it for the long haul and manage your expectations.

"Watching individual stocks in your portfolio go up can be exhilarating, but it can also be scary when you see something go down. What I really want to drive home is that even when you've bought a stock that is not performing and you have to sell it for less than you bought it for—a worst-case scenario for many—you probably aren't in as much trouble as you think. First of all, the way our tax system is set up, selling stocks at a loss gives you a chance to offset other stock gains. This is useful if you have capital gains from other transactions, which are taxed at a higher rate than your regular income. So you may not have lost as much as you think.

"Second, you want your portfolio to be diverse enough that, no, you're not going up all the time. Each component in your portfolio provides balance. You don't know what's going to happen next. War may break out in some part of the globe that provides a key component for the tech industry, for instance, and suddenly an entire sector is in turmoil. Or something happens that makes Americans dial down their spending and suddenly our consumer economy is thrown out of whack. These are macro-level events, some happening on a world stage, and you're not in control of them. What you can control, however, is being invested across the board so that uncertainty in one arena doesn't suddenly dry up your dividends or make your entire portfolio tumble.

"Every so often, you need to check your stocks to make sure your predictions are in accordance with reality. Re-evaluate, rebalance, but don't think you're doing it wrong just because some stocks go down and others go up. Over the long term, the stock market delivers returns that beat inflation, and that is its strength. Just mimicking it can give you a foundation to increase your wealth.

"Finally, after extolling what I truly believe is the best economic system in the world, urging you to use your assets, and, I hope, convincing you to give both real estate and the stock market a try, where do I think the most potential for profit comes from? The answer is: I believe with all my heart that it comes from investing—not in stocks or bonds, but in yourself.

"This is important, I really want you to hear this. I believe your strongest asset is your own expertise. Your ingenuity. Doing the hard work to get to the top of whatever game you want to play. You can use your skills to find ways to make more money, no matter what your profession may be. There will only ever be one *you* in the world. Make the most of that uniqueness—I really think it's a crime not to. Use your abilities to the fullest; there is always another hill to conquer.

"Nowhere is that more true than in retirement. Retirement is actually a relatively new idea, the idea that at fifty-five or sixty you should simply stop doing what you've been doing for the last thirty or forty years—who came up with that? Of course, it used to be that we only lived to be around sixty years old. Now, we're just getting started.

"On one hand, it's a burden to have to figure out ways to save enough that you can support thirty years of living expenses when you're no longer bringing in a salary. It's a challenge, as many of you have discovered, but it's not insurmountable. The earlier you start planning for it, the better off you'll be. But equally important is planning how you'll spend your time.

"Men, in particular, tend to define themselves in their workplaces; traditionally, that's where their sense of self comes from, their job title. It's also where they have the most social interactions and sense of accomplishment. Suddenly, from one day to the next, having all of that taken away when you retire—that can be a real jolt to the system. Men who can't figure out what else to do with their lives tend to have very poor health outcomes within a year or two of retirement. In this case, failing to plan for how you'll live can translate into not living very long at all.

"Women tend to have a different set of problems, as they are often juggling a 'second shift' at home. But while their whole identity may not be tangled up in their work, they usually don't make as much money as men do, and consequently haven't been able to save as much for retirement.

"Again, planning early, investing in yourself, and being creative in how you construct your life post-retirement . . . all of those things come into play. For both genders, retirement can be a time to try new adventures, take on new projects, make a difference in your families and communities. I want you to reconsider what is possible, and I hope this cruise has given you a taste of what that can look like.

"In our own lives, we go through economic and personal cycles of ups and downs, much like the national and global economies. Stay optimistic. It takes stamina, it takes persistence, but take a long view. Set out to accomplish great things, whatever that looks like to you, and enjoy the ride.

"When you think about the most memorable times in your life, graduations would probably make the list. A graduation is a celebration of what we have accomplished and a door opening to a new future. It is also a time when we say goodbye not just to our friends, perhaps, but to the person we used to be. We know in our hearts that someone stronger, more accomplished, more able to make a difference in the world is being born. In this sense, retirement is just another graduation: a gangway to the next enriching destination on your journey.

"I have enjoyed the opportunity to work with you all, to pass on my experiences and advice. I know I speak for Gunnar and Rachael in wishing you every success and every happiness as you embark on your next great adventure."

End of the Day

After dinner, the couples felt restless. No one wanted to spend their last night just sitting around talking; to some extent, they felt talked out. Although they had enjoyed the cruise, they were ready to go home and start putting some of William, Rachael, and Gunnar's advice into practice.

They decided to head for the lounge to see if the piano player was playing. What they found instead was a big band in full swing. Delighted, the couples took to the dance floor. They stayed up far later than any of them had intended. It was the perfect end to a fun and enlightening cruise.

CHAPTER TEN

FAREWELLS

The Morning Ritual

For their last morning on the cruise, the couples decided to meet for coffee and pastries in the lounge before they had to disembark. They were still a little tired from dancing the night before, but they also felt rejuvenated from the cruise and excited by all they had learned. They exchanged business cards and email addresses, and texted each other their phone numbers. As promised, Betty had created an online document of her notes and each person had added things they had learned; everyone would be able to read it when they got home.

"I can't believe the cruise is over," Betty said. "I'm a little teary. I feel like we've all become such good friends."

"That's true," agreed Shirley. "I'll miss all of you."

"You won't miss me," Lamont laughed. "We already have a call set up to start talking about our line of greeting cards."

"That's right," said Peter. "This isn't really an ending. It's a chance for new beginnings."

"Isn't that what retirement is?" asked Joe. "I mean, I always used to think of it as the end of the line in a way—the end of my working days. But it's really the beginning of a whole new chapter of life."

"It's exciting," agreed Betty. "We have this wonderful opportunity to decide on purpose how we want to live the next stage of our lives."

Gabriela nodded. "I always thought planning for retirement just meant socking money away for later. I didn't realize how important it was to figure out our goals and to make a plan to support them."

"It feels a lot less scary after everything we've learned here," said Sam. "In fact, Shirley and I are looking forward to taking Gunnar's advice and seeing what we can do with our duplex."

"Sam is even thinking about parlaying it into a place with more apartments," Shirley added, "but I'm not sold on the idea."

"She's not sold *yet*," said Sam. "And I'm not saying we'll do it tomorrow. But if there's one thing I've learned on this cruise, it's that there's a lot more to learn than I ever dreamed of."

"Part of believing in yourself means believing you can find the answers," Maya said. "William steered us in the right direction—if you'll pardon the nautical pun!—and now it's up to us to, well, stay afloat!"

With that, the captain announced that it was time to start disembarkation. With a sense that they had graduated, the couples gave each other final hugs and promises to keep in touch.

Then they left the ship—some to explore New Orleans, others to catch an early flight home—but all of them with a newfound sense of purpose as they contemplated their own golden years.

CHAPTER ELEVEN

REFIRING

Betty and Joe

In the weeks following the cruise, Betty and Joe began their retirement transition in earnest. They decided that Gunnar was right—it was smarter for Betty to continue to work for another five years. This allowed them to keep their health insurance through her employer until they were both eligible for Medicare. It also meant they had a little more money coming in that they could invest with. Neither Betty nor Joe had much interest in picking stocks or playing the market, so they decided to open an account with an online broker and pick a couple of different mutual funds—one that mirrored the Russell 3000 Index and another that had a more global perspective—and arranged to automatically invest a small amount every month.

It was a little more difficult to figure out how they would live on $100,000 a year when they had been living on $142,000. They wanted to be able to stay in their house and they were ambivalent about having a college student living with them, even in the attic apartment Joe had renovated for their son. They decided to give it a try for the coming school year, just to see if it was worth doing. Betty spruced up the room and put up fliers on the bulletin board at the local college, specifying that the lease was for the school year only. They got five calls within the first day and ultimately rented the room to a quiet graduate student from Belize who was delighted not to have to worry about subletting or being on the hook for rent during the summer months.

Joe was interested in doing handyman work around the neighborhood, but their younger son offered to help him sell handmade products on Etsy instead. Together, they decided Joe should specialize in building shelves for tools. It was something he had done for his own workshop and had refined over the years; plus he enjoyed it and could see there was a market for it. With his son's help, he built a few prototypes, took some pictures, and set up an online store. He quickly found himself in demand, so much so that he was able to raise his prices a little. It didn't match what he'd made when he was working, but it did help them smooth over the sudden drop in income now that he'd retired.

Joe also started working in the garden. He remembered the Myrtles Plantation and how peaceful he had felt touring the gardens. With Betty's blessing, he dug up a chunk of the backyard and put in raised beds. He also created a compost heap for them to turn kitchen scraps into healthy soil for the plants. Both his sons came over to help him build a small cold frame greenhouse so he had a place to give seedlings an early start for next year. Planning and building the garden gave Joe a chance to work with his sons, and it also gave him something to look forward to. Betty had been right: Some things were valuable even if they weren't moneymaking schemes, and Joe knew she was as excited about how happy gardening made him as she was about the prospect of homegrown vegetables and herbs to cook with next summer.

Betty, meanwhile, had started looking into tutoring after school. There were a number of public and private high schools in her area, and she knew many of the English teachers in both. She had cards printed up with her name, her phone number, and "Tutor: AP English Language and Lit," and gave them out to her colleagues, who were happy to refer her to families looking for extra help. Focusing on tutoring for the Advanced Placement exam meant that she wouldn't have many students early in the school year, when she was setting up her own classes and getting to know her students, but it did mean she would be extra busy in the second half of the year. Betty figured this was a good opportunity to find out how many students she could handle tutoring on the side as well as build her reputation as a tutor before she retired from the classroom.

She also started talking to some friends about creating a nonprofit that offered free tutoring to kids who needed but couldn't afford the extra help. Several of her colleagues in different fields were enthusiastic, and Betty decided to move forward with creating a board and filing for nonprofit status. She felt a real sense of pride in coming up with this way to be able to give back and support the children in her community.

Finally, Joe decided he would take his social security payments as soon as he was eligible, at sixty-two. That extra money would also help as they navigated retirement, and hopefully it would mean Betty could wait until she was a little older to take her social security—the longer she waited, the more the monthly payout would be. They also talked to their sons about a reverse mortgage; they wanted them to know that it meant at some point, the house would be sold. Both of their sons were happy that their parents had a way to be able to afford to stay in their home, and the boys were both building their own careers and families; neither one was planning to move back in with their folks. Joe and Betty wouldn't be eligible for a HECM for another couple of years, but they felt having an additional source of monthly income would take the pressure off having to rent out a room or continuing to work if their health suddenly changed. And it made it possible for them to think about traveling a little or even taking another cruise.

All in all, Betty and Joe implemented much of the advice they'd been given and felt a lot more confident about their future.

Shirley and Sam

Shirley and Sam were not only excited to see their friends Joe and Betty making such immediate headway—they were also inspired to make some changes themselves.

The first thing they did was make a list of all the deferred maintenance they needed to do on their own home and on the duplex. Sam took on the job of researching what different rentals went for in their area and discovered they were renting their duplex on the lower end of the market. He also toured multiunit properties that were available for sale, just to see what other landlords were doing and how possible it might be for them to buy a six- or eight-unit property. Shirley was a little reluctant to take on a bigger debt, so Sam was determined to do as much research as was needed to make sure they made a good decision.

Shirley also moved forward with her idea for a line of greeting cards. She and Lamont worked together virtually until they had a dozen cards they were proud of. The cards were visually beautiful thanks to Lamont's design talents, and both funny and heart-warming, thanks to Shirley's writing. Maya helped them write up a partnership agreement. They invested in some printing costs, and Shirley began to feature the cards at her shop. Sam also helped get the word out, letting friends and colleagues know about his wife's cards, and they ended up distributing the cards in boutiques around the country. It brought in a small but steady income and gave Shirley so much creative joy. She and Lamont began talking about expanding the line as well as writing a children's book together using some of the characters they had created for the cards.

Sam and Shirley also sat down and ruthlessly started going through their expenses. They decided that for the next year, their focus would be on stashing as much money as they could in savings. Sam wanted to follow Gunnar's advice and aggressively pay down the mortgage on the duplex so he could parlay the equity into a down payment on another rental property. Shirley still wasn't sold on the idea of getting another rental, largely because so much of the day-to-day with renters fell to her when Sam was on the road. But she did agree that having a bigger nest egg was important, whether they ended up investing in real estate, the stock market, or even expanding her own business.

They went over their credit card bills and made a real budget for the first time in years. They agreed to cut out everything that wasn't necessary, but instead of thinking of it as depriving themselves of fun, they reminded each other frequently that what they were really doing was building their future. They tackled the most urgent maintenance on the house and duplex first, and when one tenant left, they took the opportunity to make some improvements and repaint the interior. To their amazement, they found they were able to rent it out again quickly and for more money.

Sam's research and their elbow grease were already paying off. After that, Shirley agreed that she and Sam should learn more about what it takes to do well in real estate.

Peter and Rose

Peter and Rose returned from the cruise with a new frame of mind. They realized the most important thing for them was creating memories for themselves and their family while Rose was still healthy enough to participate. The first thing they both did was make sure their estate was in order. They wrote and signed their wills, gave their son a power of attorney for their health, and left documents outlining what they wanted for a memorial service if something should happen to either of them. They each also created a folder with all of their critical information: phone numbers of people to contact, passwords to their phones and personal accounts, and where to find important papers.

The sale of their company went through and they followed Gunnar's advice, setting up a series of trusts for their grandchildren and for their own investments. After that, they made plans to enjoy life to the fullest. Rose planned a family trip to Italy and they went over the winter break. Her son and his family were able to join them and they had a magical time, especially in Florence, Venice, and Rome. During the trip, both Peter and Rose discovered a tremendous love for traveling.

Peter was particularly glad that they had taken the trip when they did. Rose's health began to decline in February, and by May, she had passed away. Peter felt at peace knowing she had spent her last months enjoying life and spending so much time with the people she loved.

He ended up selling their house after Rose passed away and renting a studio apartment closer to his son. This forced him to go through his possessions and donate, give away, or sell most of the things that had collected over the years. He didn't resent it, however; Peter kept a few pieces that reminded him of his late wife, and the rest he was happy to send on to a new home.

Over the summer, he spent a lot of time with his grandchildren, while he spent the colder months traveling to visit friends all over the world. It was a lifestyle he had never imagined for himself, and he credited the cruise with pushing him to make decisions and try new things. It had opened up a world of possibility.

Gabriela and Lamont

Soon after the cruise, Lamont and Gabriela set aside an entire weekend to plan out their future. They used the shorthand of "just right" to remind them of the Three Bears and Goldilocks' bowl of porridge in ice, and how much more important it was that they create a life that worked for them rather than one dictated by what other people thought or did.

Gabriela decided to create a series of online classes, branded with the name of her company, to teach some of the skills they encouraged in the temps who worked for them. She began a podcast interviewing other small business owners about their journeys and what they looked for in their workforce. She also wrote articles for trade newsletters and the occasional magazine. She reached out to her alumni associations for both undergrad and graduate school, and was booked to give talks to a variety of alumni groups.

Gabriela also started to take advantage of the 401(k) program she had set up for her employees. In addition, she and Lamont decided to work with a broker and committed to putting a set amount every month into a well-balanced stock portfolio. The two of them began by researching companies they liked and keeping a watch list, and they slowly developed a true enjoyment of the stock market.

Lamont, meanwhile, decided to devote a certain percentage of his time each week to developing new clients, and another chunk of time to working on his own original projects. He and Gabriela had agreed to leave work behind at least three evenings a week and one full weekend day, which meant there were times he could no longer squeeze in all the clients who wanted to work with him. Although he found it very difficult, Lamont began to say no to the clients who really weren't a good fit for him. He also began working with another freelancer as part of his virtual team, each of them bringing the other in to work on parts of projects that were better suited to their strengths. Instead of his income going down, Lamont was astonished to see that his income actually went up once he began saying no. Also, once he began to focus on the things he did particularly well, he realized he could raise his rates and still be competitive in his niche.

They did redo their living room, but on a shoestring budget; they took the money they had put aside for the remodel and launched their stock portfolio instead. They used paint Lamont had left over from a project he'd finished the year before, which had just been sitting in their garage, to repaint the walls a vibrant color. They rearranged the furniture to give the house more of a sense of flow, and invested in simple but comfortable throw cushions, which Gabriela took to embroidering while they relaxed in the evening, teasing her husband that he was no longer the only artist in the family.

Finally, although they discussed paying their mortgage down early, they felt their money was working harder for them in the stock market. They decided to refinance the house, locking in a lower interest rate.

Maya and Andrei

Even before the cruise ended, Maya and Andrei realized the most important contribution it had made to their lives was that it got them to think and talk to each other about the future again. They had spent the last several years exhausted from the demands of a young family, a new business, and tight money; mostly, they talked to each other about how to get through the day or the week. Now, they realized how important it was for them to envision a future they could work toward together.

They got their wills in order and bought life insurance. As soon as they did that, Maya felt a tremendous weight lift off her shoulders. She hadn't realized how much she had been worrying in the back of her mind about what might happen until the safety net was in place. Andrei talked to his business partner about adding a 401(k) to the company, explaining to him the importance of taking care of their future while they had time on their side. It took some convincing, but they did it and discovered that having a 401(k) allowed them to attract even better talent to the company once they started hiring.

Andrei also committed to being more present with his children. He realized this was one journey he really wanted to enjoy. He arranged his work schedule so that he could take on the morning routine every day, which gave them all some stability, and on the two days a week he worked from home, he took off the afternoons to spend with the kids, catching up on emails and paperwork at night after Maya got home. It felt a little like tag team, but they made it work.

Maya's part-time schedule was three days a week and she went into work early each day, using that time to talk to the other attorneys and the staff and really get a feel for what the practice was like and how she might grow there. She quickly realized it was not a good fit for her; the partners were very set in their ways and there was little room for her to grow. She began to use the time the kids were in school on the days she was off from work to network and look for another job, and by the following year, it had paid off: Maya landed a full-time position with a pharmaceutical company for better pay, more interesting work, and a clear path for advancement.

Andrei, meanwhile, parlayed his own expertise into a side business, consulting with other entrepreneurs in the software industry. He and Maya continued to rent, but they became serious about putting money aside, not just for retirement, but for their children's education as well. They felt more united as a couple now that they had a shared vision for their future. They were on the same team once more.

TEN FINAL THOUGHTS

1. Don't become anxious. You have options.

2. Don't jump into unfamiliar ventures. Do your research, and if you can start by dipping your toe in the water, do.

3. Don't get into the latest craze. The fear of missing out can cause you to make poor decisions.

4. Don't deal with strangers. Take the time to get to know someone. Trust, but verify.

5. Don't make hasty decisions. Be particularly wary of anyone who tries to pressure you into a snap decision.

6. Be patient. You didn't get into a financial pickle overnight; you won't get out of one overnight either.

7. Be comfortable in your own backyard. Live the life you want to live. It's all about the journey.

8. Be aware of schemes. If it sounds too good to be true, it likely isn't true.

9. Be thankful for what you have.

10. Be kind to others.

Wishing you every success in your own golden years,

—Robert Barbera

About the Author

Robert Barbera is a proud Italian American. His immigrant parents taught him the value of hard work and the importance of family. He made his first stock investment in 1954, only four years out of high school, and bought his first building in 1961. Through hard work, dedication, focus, and the support of his family, he now has 500 units and multiple subsidiary companies, making real estate the cornerstone of his success.

Throughout his life, Robert has built wealth not just for himself and his family, but also for many other people in fields as diverse as restaurants, car dealerships, and the financial industry. He launched The Barbera Foundation in 1994 and has donated his time, expertise, and financial resources to many worthy organizations, including Pepperdine University, Thomas Aquinas College, and the California State University system.

Robert was lucky in love, having had a happy, forty-five-year marriage to his late wife, Bernice, and finding love a second time around with Josephine, whom he married in 2003. He is the father of three wonderful children, Ann, John, and Patricia, and the grandfather of seven.

The Mentoris Project represents a piece of Robert's legacy. It connects his past, his parents, his children, and the future by honoring the achievements of Italians and Italian Americans and publishing inspirational books. Learn more at: www.mentorisproject.org

ACKNOWLEDGMENTS

After working with Laura Brennan on two books about wealth development—*Building Wealth* and *Building Wealth 101*—who else would I call to help me with my third? Laura finessed my metaphors of boating and water and turned my rough manuscript into a great read. Laura always understands what is needed and I am deeply grateful to have had the opportunity to collaborate with her yet again.

Many others have helped along the way. But if it weren't for Karen Richardson who manages the Mentoris Project, the series would not have been possible.

ALSO FROM THE MENTORIS PROJECT

America's Forgotten Founding Father
A Novel Based on the Life of Filippo Mazzei
by Rosanne Welch, PhD

A. P. Giannini—Il Banchiere di Tutti
di Francesca Valente

A. P. Giannini—The People's Banker
by Francesca Valente

The Architect Who Changed Our World
A Novel Based on the Life of Andrea Palladio
by Pamela Winfrey

At Last
A Novel Based on the Life of Harry Warren
by Stacia Raymond

A Boxing Trainer's Journey
A Novel Based on the Life of Angelo Dundee
by Jonathan Brown

Breaking Barriers
A Novel Based on the Life of Laura Bassi
by Jule Selbo

Building Heaven's Ceiling
A Novel Based on the Life of Filippo Brunelleschi
by Joe Cline

The Embrace of Hope
A Novel Based on the Life of Frank Capra
by Kate Fuglei

The Faithful
A Novel Based on the Life of Giuseppe Verdi
by Collin Mitchell

Fermi's Gifts
A Novel Based on the Life of Enrico Fermi
by Kate Fuglei

First Among Equals
A Novel Based on the Life of Cosimo de' Medici
by Francesco Massaccesi

The Flesh and the Spirit
A Novel Based on the Life of St. Augustine of Hippo
by Sharon Reiser and Ali A. Smith

God's Messenger
A Novel Based on the Life of Mother Frances X. Cabrini
by Nicole Gregory

Grace Notes
A Novel Based on the Life of Henry Mancini
by Stacia Raymond

Guido's Guiding Hand
A Novel Based on the Life of Guido d'Arezzo
by Kingsley Day

Harvesting the American Dream
A Novel Based on the Life of Ernest Gallo
by Karen Richardson

Humble Servant of Truth
A Novel Based on the Life of Thomas Aquinas
by Margaret O'Reilly

The Judicious Use of Intangibles
A Novel Based on the Life of Pietro Belluschi
by W.A.W. Parker

Leonardo's Secret
A Novel Based on the Life of Leonardo da Vinci
by Peter David Myers

Little by Little We Won
A Novel Based on the Life of Angela Bambace
by Peg A. Lamphier, PhD

The Making of a Prince
A Novel Based on the Life of Niccolò Machiavelli
by Maurizio Marmorstein

A Man of Action Saving Liberty
A Novel Based on the Life of Giuseppe Garibaldi
by Rosanne Welch, PhD

Marconi and His Muses
A Novel Based on the Life of Guglielmo Marconi
by Pamela Winfrey

No Person Above the Law
A Novel Based on the Life of Judge John J. Sirica
by Cynthia Cooper

The Pirate Prince of Genoa
A Novel Based on the Life of Admiral Andrea Doria
by Maurizio Marmorstein

Relentless Visionary: Alessandro Volta
by Michael Berick

Ride Into the Sun
A Novel Based on the Life of Scipio Africanus
by Patric Verrone

Rita Levi-Montalcini
Pioneer & Ambassador of Science
by Francesca Valente

Saving the Republic
A Novel Based on the Life of Marcus Cicero
by Eric D. Martin

The Seven Senses of Italy
by Nicole Gregory

Sinner, Servant, Saint
A Novel Based on the Life of St. Francis of Assisi
by Margaret O'Reilly

Soldier, Diplomat, Archaeologist
A Novel Based on the Bold Life of Louis Palma di Cesnola
by Peg A. Lamphier, PhD

The Soul of a Child
A Novel Based on the Life of Maria Montessori
by Kate Fuglei

What a Woman Can Do
A Novel Based on the Life of Artemisia Gentileschi
by Peg A. Lamphier, PhD

The Witch of Agnesi
A Novel Based on the Life of Maria Agnesi
by Eric D. Martin

For more information on these titles and the Mentoris Project, please visit
www.mentorisproject.org

Made in the USA
Middletown, DE
28 September 2022

11436056R00120